Clear Grammar 3

Clear Grammar 3

Activities for Spoken and Written Communication

Keith S. Folse

Ann Arbor

THE UNIVERSITY OF MICHIGAN PRESS

2010   2009   2008   2007   7   6   5   4

Unit opening illustrations by Barbara Goodsitt

ISBN 978-0-472-08373-2

Acknowledgments

I would like to thank the numerous professionals who gave their expert advice in the design of the grammar presentations and some of the activities used in this textbook. Among these professionals, I would especially like to acknowledge members of TESLMW-L (the materials writers group on the TESL-L electronic communication list) who offered suggestions. Both TESL-L and TESLMW-L have proven time and time again to be excellent sources of new teaching ideas and techniques.

Special thanks go to the professionals at ESL programs at the following schools who contributed ideas and suggestions for the design and content of this book: American Language Academy (Seattle), American Language Academy (Tampa), ELS (Seattle), Houston Community College, Loyola University (New Orleans), Oregon State University (Corvallis), San Francisco State University, Spring Hill College (Mobile, AL), Tulane University (New Orleans), the University of Central Florida (Orlando), the University of Monterrey (Mexico), the University of North Texas (Denton), the University of South Florida (Tampa), the University of Southern Mississippi (Hattiesburg), the University of Washington (Seattle), and Valencia Community College (Orlando).

Finally, I would like to thank the staff of the University of Michigan Press who have worked with me on this project, particularly Mary Erwin and Kelly Sippell.

Contents

To the Teacher

Clear Grammar 3 is part of a three-volume series of grammar books for beginning to low-intermediate level students of English as a second or foreign language. Book 3 covers grammar points for intermediate nonnative learners of English, including phrasal verbs, past progressive tense, present perfect tense, adverbs of manner and related terms, verb-preposition and adjective-preposition combinations, passive voice, relative clauses, infinitives and gerunds, connectors, and verbs with direct or indirect objects.

Clear Grammar 1 contains presentations and exercises on basic grammar points such as the verb *to be,* regular verbs, simple question and negative forms, and prepositions. *Clear Grammar 2* continues this series with articles, *be going to,* irregular past tense, *how* questions, adverbs of frequency, object pronouns, *one* and *other,* possessive, comparison and superlative, modals, and problem words.

Clear Grammar 3 contains exercises that provide relevant practice in the basic grammar points for intermediate students of English as a second language (ESL). It assumes that the student has a fair reading and writing ability in English. It is designed to be used by adult learners, that is, high school age and up. It is suitable for either intensive or nonintensive programs.

An important feature of this book is the number and variety of types of exercises included. Teachers and learners need a large number of practices. A plus of this book is that it contains approximately 175 exercises and activities. Furthermore, whenever possible, two smaller exercises have been included instead of one long exercise so that one may be done in class with the teacher's guidance and the other can be sent home for independent learning. A second advantage of this book is the variety of types of practice exercises and learning activities. For example, approximately 20 percent of the exercises are speaking or some type of interaction activities. Some grammar points can be practiced at the single-sentence level while other points may be learned better if seen within a larger context.

A strong attempt has been made to provide engaging activities in addition to the traditional single sentences with one blank. To this end, the written exercises are proportionally divided between sentence-level exercises and multisentence- and dialogue-level activities. Therefore, the resultant structure of this book is approximately 20 percent speaking/interactive exercises, 40 percent single-sentence practices, and 40 percent multisentence or minidialogue activities.

These last figures clearly illustrate an extremely important difference between the Clear Grammar series and other grammar books. While some grammar ESL books have included some speaking activities and others have included a few multisentence exercises, the three books in this series make use of contextualized exercises where possible. These features represent current views toward the learning of grammar in a second language, namely, that speaking practice is as important as written practice and that some grammar points are more apparent to students when these points are seen within a real and somewhat longer context.

Because learners learn in different ways based on their individual learner differences, the presentation of grammar in this series, and especially in this volume, has been varied to include both traditional deductive and inductive presentations. In the deductive presentations (see unit 6), the grammar rules are stated explicitly, and then learners work exercises that help solidify the stated patterns in their minds. In the inductive presentations (see unit 3), on the other hand, learners are given correct examples and incorrect examples of the grammar and are told to figure out the grammatical patterns and exceptions. This presentation is also followed by a series of written exercises and speaking activities that gradually become more difficult.

Clear Grammar 3 has six main goals:

1. to teach the basic grammar points necessary for intermediate ESL students;
2. to provide ample written practice in these structures at the single-sentence level as well as at the multisentence and dialogue levels;
3. to provide a wide array of practices at varying cognitive levels (i.e., not just knowledge and comprehension but also synthesis and evaluation);
4. to provide oral communication work practicing these structures through a variety of activities and games;
5. to provide ample opportunities for students to check their progress while studying these structures; and
6. to serve as a grammar reference that is written with language and terms that an intermediate-level ESL student can understand without a great deal of teacher assistance.

Clear Grammar 3 consists of twelve units. Unit 1 is a review of the basic grammatical structures covered in *Clear Grammar 2.* Unit 12 is a review unit of the material in *Clear Grammar 3*. Each of the other ten units covers a single grammar area, but sometimes a particular area may have several subdivisions. An example is unit 4, "Present Perfect Tense," in which seven usages of this tense are covered. Another example is unit 2, "Phrasal Verbs," which teaches three classes of phrasal verbs.

The units may be taught in any order. However, it is recommended that the general sequencing of the units be followed whenever possible. An attempt has been made to recycle material from one unit into following units where appropriate. For example, once present perfect tense has been covered, many of the sentences in subsequent exercises in other units include present perfect tense for further reinforcement.

Though a great deal of variety of material exists in the book, there is a general pattern within each unit. The units begin with some kind of grammar presentation. Sometimes this presentation is inductive; other times it is deductive. This presentation is then followed by a list of the most likely mistakes (i.e., potential problems) for each structure. This is followed by a series of written exercises arranged from least to most cognitively demanding. After the written work are one or more speaking activities. This is followed by a multiple choice quiz. At the end of each unit there are a review test and a list of suggestions for possible writing practice. The exact guidelines for each class (e.g., amount of writing expected of students and the exact form in which they should prepare writing exercises—handwritten or typed, single or double spaced, etc.) are left completely up to the individual instructor, as no one knows the specific teaching situation better than that teacher.

A unique feature of all three volumes of the Clear Grammar series is the inclusion of Challenge Boxes. Each Challenge Box presents a single question that requires a higher level of knowledge and understanding of the particular grammar point. Sometimes the Challenge Box requires learners to analyze the most difficult item in the previous exercise. Other times the Challenge Box presents a new item that is more difficult than the items in the previous exercise. In both cases, the purpose of this activity is twofold: (1) to raise students' understanding of the grammar point by dealing with a very difficult question about the grammatical point, and (2) to motivate the better students who might not have been challenged sufficiently by the previous exercise.

General Lesson Format

1. Grammar Presentation

   These presentations vary in method. In some units, they are deductive; in others, inductive; and in others, consciousness raising. L2 learners have a wide range of learner styles and employ an even greater range of learner strategies. It is believed that having a variety of presentation types for the grammatical structures is therefore advantageous.

2. List of Potential Errors with Corrections

   In this section of the unit, there is a list of several of the most commonly made errors. Following each error is the corrected form so that students can see not only what they should avoid but how it should be corrected. Our students represent a wide range of linguistic groups, and every effort has been made to take this into account in selecting which kinds of errors to include here.

3. Written Exercises

   Teachers and students want a large number of written exercises to allow for ample practice of the newly learned structure. The exercises have been sequenced so that the early exercises require only passive knowledge of the grammar point. For example, students circle one of two answers or put a check mark by the correct word. These exercises are followed by others that are more cognitively demanding and require active production of the language structure. In this way, students can comfortably move from passive knowledge to active production of a structure.

   The written exercises in this book are short enough to be done in a small amount of time, yet they are thorough enough to provide sufficient practice for the structure in question. These exercises may be done in class or as homework. Furthermore, they may be checked quickly either by individual students or by the class.

4. Speaking Activities

   Each unit has at least one (and often several) speaking activities. The design of these speaking activities is based on second language acquisition research by C. Doughty, M. Long, T. Pica, and P. Porter showing that certain types of activities encourage L2 learners to produce a greater amount and a higher quality of language.

   The instructions for these activities are clearly written at the top of the exercise. Students are almost always directed to work with a partner. In this case, it is important for the teacher to make sure that students do not see their partner's material ahead of time as this will not facilitate speaking. (However, not all speaking activities are set up in this manner. See the directions for the individual exercises for further clarification.)

5. Multiple Choice Exercise

   Because students often have such a hard time with this particular format and because it is similar to the format found on many standardized language tests, each unit includes an eight-question multiple choice exercise. It is important to discuss not only why the correct answers are correct but also why the distractors are not correct.

6. Review Test

   Equally as important as the teaching of a given grammar point is the measurement of the learning that has taken place. To this end, the last exercise in every unit is a review test. This review test has several *very* different kinds of questions on it. For example, one kind of question may require a simple completion while another may require error identification. This variety allows all students an opportunity to demonstrate their knowledge without interference caused by the type of question.

7. Extended Writing Activity

   At the end of each unit is a suggestion for a writing activity. The nature of the exact assignment is left up to the individual teacher. It should be noted that the main purpose of this writing activity is to incorporate yet another of the four skills in the learning of grammar.

Answer Key

In the back of the book, there is a section that contains the answers for all exercises in this text. These answers are provided so that students may check to see if their answers are correct. It is supposed that students will use the answer key after they have actually done the exercises. It is further hoped that students will use the answer key to detect their mistakes and then return to the exercises to discover the source of their error. The answer key also makes it possible for students engaged in independent study to use this workbook.

Grammar Terminology

In this book, grammar is not viewed as a theoretical science that requires complex terminology. Surely the main purpose of studying grammar in a foreign language is to be able to function better in that language, that is, to produce *accurate* communication (not just communication). To that end, the main focus of the presentations in this book is on being able to use English accurately and not on learning labels that are of little use. However, this does not mean that terminology is or should be avoided. Terms such as *phrasal verbs* and *gerunds* are introduced and explained. However, grammar terminology is only introduced when it is necessary. Furthermore, when it is introduced, explanations have been simplified to reflect the level of the learner's English ability. Complex grammar terminology serves no justifiable purpose and is to be avoided at all costs in good ESL classes and materials.

Using This Book in Your Curriculum

The number of hours needed to complete this book depends to a large extent on the students in your class. Some groups may need up to 60 hours to finish all the material, while a more advanced group might be able to omit certain units and do more work as homework, therefore using less class time. In this case, the students could finish the material in approximately 35 hours. The results of the diagnostic test (at the end of the book) can help you decide which units, if any, can be omitted or should be assigned as homework to certain students only in order to use group class time the most effectively.

Another factor that will greatly influence the number of class hours needed to complete this material successfully is whether or not the oral activities are done in class. It is recommended that teachers make every effort to do these speaking fluency activities in order to build up students' speaking ability and their confidence in their ability to use spoken English. An instructor in a course in which time is an important factor may want to consider ways of correcting student homework (e.g., posting homework answer sheets on the wall) that are less time consuming rather than omitting the speaking fluency activities.

A diagnostic test is included at the back of the book. More information about this test is given in the next section. In order to make the best use of (limited) class time, the results of this test can guide you in choosing which units to cover and which units to omit if necessary.

About the Diagnostic Test

The diagnostic test is printed on perforated pages. Have the students remove this test and take it at the first class meeting. The test consists of twenty-two questions, two for each of the eleven units. (The twelfth unit of the book is a review of the entire book, and thus no question matches it solely.) The test is set up in two parts, each part consisting of eleven questions. You may set your own time limit, but a recommended time limit is twenty minutes for all twenty-two questions. (Answers are not provided.)

The scoring for the test is fairly straightforward. On the test sheet, look to see for which units the student has missed both questions, for which the student has missed only one of the two questions, and for which the student has not missed either of the questions. You will need to make a composite picture of the results for your whole group. The units for which the most students have missed both questions or one question are the units that your class should focus on first.

Testing

Evaluation is extremely important in any language classroom, and it has a definite role in the grammar classroom. Frequent testing, not just major exams but small quizzes or checks, is vital to allow the learners to see what they have mastered and what still needs further work and to facilitate the teacher in gauging whether individual students have understood and retained the contents of the class.

Testing can come in many forms. Some teachers prefer cloze activities; others prefer multiple choice. Some teachers prefer discrete grammar items; others insist on context. Some include listening and/or speaking; others deal only with printed language. The most important things to keep in mind when testing are (1) students should know what kind of questions to expect, that is, they should know what they will have to do, because this affects how they should study, and (2) the test should test what was taught and nothing else. This second point is the mark of a good test and is essential to the fair treatment of the students.

About the Final Test

In addition to the diagnostic test, there is a final test on page 209. This is meant to be done toward the end of the course when most, if not all, of the book has been covered. This test is also printed on perforated pages and should be removed early in the course to prevent students from looking ahead. For this reason, some teachers will have students remove this test at the first class meeting and then collect these tests. It is not recommended that the results of this particular test be used as the sole deciding factor in whether a student moves from one level or course to the next. This is especially true if you have not had your students answer this type of question during the course. In general, this type of test is more difficult than regular multiple choice or cloze, and any student who scores at least 70 percent is probably ready to move on to a higher level of grammar study.

This test has two parts, each of which has the same directions. Students are to find the grammatical error in each sentence and correct it. Each of the two parts has eleven sentences, one sentence for each of the units in the book (except the final review unit, of course). The questions are in numerical order matching the corresponding units in the book. Thus, question number 7 in each part deals with material found in unit 7. It is possible to give the first part of this quiz as a progress check midway through the course and then to give the other half at the end to compare results. Again, it is not recommended that any decision regarding promotion to the next level of study be based solely on the results of this single exam.

References

Doughty, C., and T. Pica. 1986. "Information gap" tasks: do they facilitate second language acquisition? *TESOL Quarterly* 20:305–25.

Long, M. 1989. Task, group, and task-group interactions. Paper delivered at RELC Regional Seminar, Singapore.

Long, M., and P. Porter. 1985. Group work, interlanguage talk, and second language acquisition. *TESOL Quarterly* 19: 207–28.

Pica, T., and C. Doughty. 1985. Input and interaction in the communicative language classroom: a comparison of teacher fronted and group activities. In Susan M. Gass and Carolyn G. Madden, eds., *Input in Second Language Acquisition* (Rowley, MA: Newbury House).

Pica, T., and C. Doughty. 1985. The role of group work in classroom second language acquisition. *Studies in Second Language Acquisition* 7:233–48.

Unit 1

Review of Book 2

1. articles
2. *be going to* + VERB
3. irregular past tense
4. *how* questions
5. adverbs of frequency
6. object pronouns

7. *one* and *other*
8. possessive
9. comparative and superlative
10. modals
11. problem words

Exercise 1.   Articles. Write *a, an, the,* or — on the line.

Situation 1.   In this conversation, a clerk and a customer are talking at an appliance store.

Clerk: Good afternoon. How may I help you?

Customer: I bought (1)_____ TV here last month, and now there's (2) _____ problem with my TV set.

Clerk: Can you give me some more information about (3) _____ problem?

Customer: Well, when I turn on (4)_____ TV, (5)_____ screen doesn't have any picture. It just has (6)_____ little dots or (7)_____ snow all over it.

Clerk: What else can you tell me?

Customer: I think that's all I can tell you.

Clerk: OK. You'll have to bring in your TV, and then (8)_____ repair person will look at it, because (9)_____ information that you just gave me is not enough for me to recognize (10)_____ exact problem.

Situation 2.   A teacher is explaining a geography lesson to her class.

Teacher: Please open your books to (11)_____ page 87 and look at (12)_____ map of (13)_____ North America on (14)_____ page. Who can tell me (15)_____ name of (16)_____ largest country in (17)_____ North America?

Pierre: Is it (18)_____ United States?

Teacher: No, that's not (19)_____ right answer. Many people believe that (20)_____ U.S. is (21)_____ biggest country, but that is not (22)_____ correct.

Marie: Is it (23)_____ Canada?

Teacher: Yes, Marie, that's (24)_____ correct answer. And can someone tell me (25)_____ capital of (26)_____ Canada?

Paul: I'm not sure if it's (27)_____ Toronto or (28)_____ Vancouver.

Teacher: Actually, neither of (29)_____ cities that you mentioned is (30)_____ correct response.

Marie: It's (31)_____ Ottawa.

Teacher: Yes, that's right. (32)_____ homework for tomorrow is to read (33)_____ pages 72 to 84 in (34)_____ chapter 7 and answer (35)_____ questions at (36)_____ bottom of (37)_____ last page.

Paul: Mrs. Yates, I have (38)_____ question about (39)_____ final exam (40)_____ next month.

Teacher: Paul, I'm afraid we're almost out of (41)_____ time for (42)_____ today, so would you mind if we discussed that tomorrow? If anyone has (43)_____ question about our final exam, be sure to let me know during (44)_____ tomorrow's class. OK? Don't forget (45)_____ homework for tomorrow!

Exercise 2.   Write *the* or — on the line.

1. ____ Nile River

2. ____ Mediterranean Sea

3. ____ Miami

4. ____ Korea

5. ____ Africa

6. ____ Great Lakes

7. ____ United Nations

8. ____ Netherlands

9. ____ Athens

10. ____ Philippines

11. ____ Kingdom of Saudi Arabia

12. ____ Saudi Arabia

13. ____ Mississippi (the river)

14. ____ Mississippi (the state)

15. ____ Orinoco River

16. ____ Dead Sea

17. ____ Argentina

18. ____ Atlantic Ocean

19. ____ Hilton Hotel

20. ____ Himalaya Mountains

21. ____ Mexico

22. ____ Mexico City

23. ____ Greece

24. ____ South America

25. ____ Andes Mountains

26. ____ Sahara Desert

27. ____ Gulf of Mexico

28. ____ Indonesia

29. ____ Alps

30. ____ British Columbia

Exercise 3.   Present Tense, Past Tense, Present Progressive Tense, and *be* + *going to* + VERB. Write the correct form of the verb on the line.

1. play   They _____ tennis now.

My coach _____ tennis tomorrow.

My sister never _____ tennis with me.

2. do   I _____ the homework last night.

I _____ all my homework as soon as I get home

today.

I can't go out now because I _____ my homework.

3. go   She _____ to the doctor's office tomorrow morning.

She only _____ to the doctor's office when she's very

sick.

She _____ to the doctor's office because she felt sick.

4. eat (you)   Where _____ lunch yesterday?

             Where _____ dinner when you eat out?

             Where _____ dinner tonight?

5. study   I _____ grammar now.

             I almost never _____ spelling.

             I _____ vocabulary last night before I fell asleep.

Exercise 4.   Verb Discrimination. Underline the correct form of the verb.

1. Tom and Alex (go, are going, went, are going to go) to Texas a month ago.

2. Look at the sky! It (rains, is raining, rained, is going to rain) soon.

3. Mike's not home now. Maybe he (watches, is watching, watched, is going to watch) TV at Zeke's house.

4. I can't wait to be on the beach. Just think! Another hour from now and we (are being, were, are going to be) on the beach in Florida.

5. My uncle didn't (give, gives, going to give, gave) me a birthday present this year.

6. People in France (take, are taking, are going to take, took) a long vacation in August.

7. I (need, am needing, am going to need, needed) some help tomorrow afternoon. Can you help me?

8. I had some free time last night, so I (draw, am drawing, drew, am going to draw) some pictures.

Exercise 5.   Write the past tense of these verbs.

1.	become _____	16.	sell	_____
2.	send _____	17.	have	_____
3.	break _____	18.	hear	_____
4.	bring _____	19.	sing	_____
5.	build _____	20.	hold	_____
6.	sit _____	21.	buy	_____
7.	hurt _____	22.	sleep	_____
8.	choose _____	23.	know	_____
9.	leave _____	24.	let	_____
10.	drink _____	25.	lose	_____
11.	take _____	26.	tear	_____
12.	fall _____	27.	think	_____
13.	find _____	28.	fly	_____
14.	forget _____	29.	run	_____
15.	wear _____	30.	see	_____

Exercise 6.   Fill in the missing words in these *how* questions.

1. *A:* How _____ brothers do you have?

   B: Five.

2. *A:* How _____ is Miami from here?

   B: 800 miles.

3. *A:* How _____ is Brazil?

   B: It's the fifth biggest country in the world.

4. *A:* How _____ is her house?

   B: It has 3 bedrooms and 2 bathrooms.

5. *A:* How _____ is that mountain?

   B: Over three thousand feet.

6. *A:* How _____ sugar do you want?

   B: Two tablespoons, please.

7. *A:* How _____ is that article?

    B: 16 pages.

8. *A:* How _____ do you eat out?

    B: Two or three times a week.

9. *A:* How _____ does the baby weigh?

    B: About ten pounds.

10. *A:* How _____ is your grandfather?

    B: He's ninety-seven.

Exercise 7.   Adverbs of Frequency. Underline the correct answers.

1. I (never study, study never) at the library because it (always is, is always) too quiet
    there.

2. How (usually, often, never) do you go to the post office?

3. He is such a good student that he (has hardly, hardly has) to study. He (always makes,
    makes always) good grades.

4. We rarely (eat, don't eat) breakfast together. All of us have to go to work at different
    times.

5. How (usually, often, never) do you eat scrambled eggs
    for breakfast?

6. When I was a kid, we (walked usually, usually
    walked) to school.

7. (Does Mark ever, Does ever Mark, Ever does
    Mark) play baseball after school?

8. Linda (isn't never, never isn't, isn't ever, ever
    isn't) late to class. She (is always, always is)
    right on time.

9. When I was a kid, my father and I (all of the time played baseball together, played
    baseball together all of the time).

10. I don't know why Randy is late. He doesn't (rarely, never, usually) arrive late for
    anything.

Exercise 8.   Object Pronouns. Read this short passage. There are three mistakes with pronouns. Circle the mistakes and write the correct form above the mistake.

Last year Marcelo Carrico of Italy won the World Skiing Championship. Many people were surprised when Carrico took the first prize, but I was not surprised. In fact, I expected he to win the championship because he had been practicing a lot and because he had won a few minor competitions just before the world championship. For winning the championship, Carrico won a gold medal. I have a newspaper article that shows he with the medal. In the picture, Carrico is looking at them. You can see how proud he is to have this medal. I know that him is a very good skier who will win many other medals in the future.

Speaking Activity

Exercise 9.   Speaking Activity: *One* and *Other*

Step 1.   Work with a partner. One of you is responsible for A, and the other is responsible for B.

Step 2.   Read the pair of sentences. There are an A sentence and a B sentence. Both have an underlined part. Which one is correct and which one is wrong?

Step 3.   Circle the letter of the wrong sentence and write the correct answer above. Then write your reason on the line.

Step 4.   Compare your answers. Discuss any differences. Can you both explain why you say a sentence is wrong? *Remember:* One student is responsible for explaining the A sentences, and the other student is responsible for explaining the B sentences.

1. (A) <u>Another</u> telephone numbers for the bank are 555-8584 and 555-7182.

    (B) For our next vacation, let's go to Egypt. <u>Another</u> good place might be Turkey.

    Reason: _____

2. (A) I wish I had a blue pen, but I don't have <u>it</u>.

    (B) She said the car that Pedro was driving was blue, but I didn't see <u>it</u>.

    Reason: _____

3. (A) If there are <u>other</u> students waiting, a student can only use this computer

    for an hour.

    (B) My fork was dirty, so I had to ask the waitress to bring me <u>other</u>.

    Reason: _____

4. (A) I enjoyed my trip to Vancouver last month. I'd love to go there <u>another time</u>.

    (B) Wow, that sandwich was really delicious. I'd like to eat <u>other</u>.

    Reason: _____

5. (A) There is a letter for you on the desk, and there is <u>other one</u> on the sofa.

    (B) Some people like to play golf, but <u>others</u> hate it.

    Reason: _____

6. (A) Could you please give me <u>other</u> glass of iced tea? I'm so thirsty!

    (B) The teacher was sick, so <u>another</u> teacher came to our class today.

    Reason: _____

7. (A) New cars are on sale there now. If you buy <u>one</u> before October, you

    can get a discount.

    (B) I don't know where your chemistry book is. I put <u>one</u> on the table.

    Reason: _____

8. (A) The exam had only 6 questions. The first one was easy, but <u>the another ones</u>

    were hard.

    (B) Pedro has 2 older sisters. One lives in New York, and <u>the other</u> is in Honolulu.

    Reason: _____

Exercise 10.   Possessive: Multiple Choice. Circle the letter of the correct answer.

1. "Why is that table on sale?"

    "There's a scratch on _____."

    (A) the table's top   (C) the top of the table

    (B) the top's table   (D) the table of the top

2. "Hey, are those your books?"

    "No, but they might be _____."

    (A) Tommy's books   (C) the books of Tommy

    (B) the books of Tommy's   (D) the books' Tommy

3. "_____ keys are these?"

   "Maybe they're June's."

   (A) Which　　　　　　　(C) Whom

   (B) Whose　　　　　　　(D) Who

4. "Is this your sweater?"

   "Yes, it's _____."

   (A) mine sweater　　　　(C) mine

   (B) mine one　　　　　　(D) sweater mine

5. "Did you do _____?"

   "No. I couldn't understand it."

   (A) the homework of last night　(C) the homework's last night

   (B) last night's homework　　　(D) the last night of homework

6. "Who is this next to your sister?"

   "That's my _____."

   (A) cousin's wife　　　　(C) cousin of her

   (B) cousin of my wife　　(D) wife of my cousin

7. "Did you see what Matthew bought? He has two new cats."

   "No, I haven't seen _____. What color are they?"

   (A) new cats of Matthew　　　(C) the Matthew's new cats

   (B) the new cats of Matthew　(D) Matthew's new cats

8. "Excuse me, sir. There is a green car that is blocking my car. _____ car is it?"

   "Actually, I don't have any idea at all."

   (A) Whom　　　　　　　(C) Of whose

   (B) Of whom　　　　　　(D) Whose

Exercise 11.   Comparative and Superlative. Write true sentences from the information given. Be sure to use a comparative or superlative form. Follow the examples.

1. Paris / Los Angeles / big

   <u>Los Angeles is bigger than Paris.</u>

2. Los Angeles / big / city / in the U.S.

   <u>Los Angeles is the biggest city in the U.S.</u>

3. Paris / Los Angeles / old

   _____

4. Brazil / large / country / in South America

   _____

5. This car / expensive / that car

   _____

6. August / hot / month of the year

   _____

7. A diamond / hard / mineral / on earth

   _____

8. English / Spanish / hard / to learn

   _____

Exercise 12.   Comparative and Superlative. Fill in the blanks with an appropriate word.

1. Vanilla ice cream is good, but I like chocolate more

   _____ vanilla.

2. Today's test was bad, but yesterday's test was

   _____ than today's.

3. Brazil is a big country, but Canada is

   _____. However, Russia is

   _____ country in the world.

4. Peaches are more delicious _____ apples, but the

   taste of watermelons is also _____.

5. It's two hundred miles to New York, but it's four hundred miles to Boston. If we go to Boston, then we have to drive _____.

6. Keith speaks fast, and Elena does, too. However, Irene speaks _____ of all of the teachers.

7. I don't like the color of the walls in this room. This color is not good for this room. If you paint it any new color, it will definitely look _____.

8. I only put a little salt in the soup. If you want it to taste _____, be sure to put some salt in it.

9. The question on the science test asked, "What is the name of the _____ star in the sky?"

10. If you have a car, _____ fastest way to go downtown from your apartment is to use King Street and then Gravlin Way.

Exercise 13.   Underline the correct modals.

1. *A:* (Might, Could, Should) you help me? I'm trying to find the Lawson Building.

    B: Sure. That's easy. Go back two blocks and turn right. It's right there.

    A: Wow, I walked right there, but I didn't see it.

    B: You (can, will, must) be joking. It's a huge building!

2. *A:* Welcome to Sam's Sandwiches. How (can, must, would) I help you?

    B: Let me see . . . (Could, Should, Must) I have two turkey sandwiches and a soft drink?

    A: Sure. Your total is $6.25.

    B: $6.25? The total (can, had better, should) be $5.25, right?

    A: Well, the register says $6.25. Why do you think $6.25 is wrong?

    B: Well, sandwiches are $2 each and a soft drink is $1.25. If you add that up, you (will, can, might) get $5.25.

    A: It looks like you're right. The machine (had better, will, must) be wrong. $5.25, please.

3. *A:* Mark, what does the word "tough" mean?

   B: Well, it has different meanings. It (might, had better, will) mean "not soft, difficult to cut." Or it (should, could, had better) mean "difficult to understand or do."

   A: I looked it up in my English-German dictionary, but it isn't there.

   B: Are you sure? It's a common word. It (must, can, may) be there.

   A: If I knew this word in German, then surely I (can, must, could) do this homework.

   B: Are you having problems with the homework?

   A: Actually, yes, I am. (Can, Should, Might) you help me? I'm really lost.

   B: When (will, can, would) you like me to help you?

   A: How about tomorrow after class?

   B: No, I don't think so. I (must, had better, might) have to go with my dad to the store.

   A: OK, when you know when you (can, had better, should) help me, call me and let me know.

Exercise 14. Modals. Circle the error in each sentence. Write the correction above the error.

1. Do you could help me?

2. I won't not go to the party Friday night.

3. In 1995, I could graduate from high school.

4. Could I to borrow your car tomorrow?

5. If I had a problem now, I will talk to Sallie.

6. Something's wrong. The total could be $5.80.

7. Every driver must has a valid license.

8. You ought call the store before you drive there.

9. Reading class is easy, so I must not study for it.

10. Tom maybe at school, but I'm not sure.

Exercise 15.   Problem Words. Underline the correct words.

1. Japan (is, has) a very large population.

2. He looks old, but he (has, is) only twenty-seven years old.

3. My feet hurt. I'm (very, too) tired to play tennis right now.

4. I enjoyed the movie. It was (very, too) funny.

5. I didn't buy that book at Johnson's Bookstore because it was (very, too) expensive.

6. In my country, (have, there are) many problems.

7. My country (has, there is) a large park in the middle of the capital.

8. How old (have, has, are, is) your parents?

9. The exams in our science class with Mr. Taylor (is, are) tough.

10. Shrimp and crab (doesn't have, don't have, hasn't, haven't) many calories, but (it is, they are, it has, they have) a lot of protein.

11. (Almost, Most) people in my city go to work by car.

12. My last test score was (almost, most) perfect. I made 99.

13. I need a pencil with a good eraser (to, for) my math exam tomorrow.

14. I am in this English course (to, for) improve my English.

15. You (have, are) so lucky. You only (are, have) nine students in your class. When I saw your room today, I couldn't believe it. (Almost, Most) of the desks are empty!

Extra Writing Practice

Situation: Two friends haven't seen each other in a long time. Today they ran into (met) each other at the supermarket. Write a dialogue between the two friends.

Be sure to practice several of the grammar items in this review unit. For example, the two friends might talk about why they are in the store, and one person might say, "I made some spaghetti for dinner, but I didn't have any sauce, so I came here to get some sauce for <u>the</u> spaghetti." Always underline the grammar point that you have used so the teacher can see what you are trying to practice.

Unit 2

Phrasal Verbs

1. form: VERB + PARTICLE
3. nonseparable
2. separable
4. without objects

Note: Phrasal verbs are also called two-word verbs, three-word verbs, VERB + PARTICLE, or sometimes VERB + PREPOSITION.

 **Discover Grammar**

Study these four groups of sentences. Some are marked OK and some are marked X (wrong).

Group 1.   (A) I called up my friend. (OK)
                      (B) I called up him. (X)
                      (C) I called my friend up. (OK)
                      (D) I called him up. (OK)

Group 2.   (E) Did you turn the lights on? (OK)
                      (F) Did you turn them on? (OK)
                      (G) Did you turn on the lights? (OK)
                      (H) Did you turn on them? (X)

Group 3.   (I) The teacher called on Sandra and Will. (OK)
(J) The teacher called Sandra and Will on. (X)
(K) The teacher called on them. (OK)
(L) The teacher called them on. (X)

This unit deals with **phrasal verbs.** The phrasal verbs here are *call up, turn on,* and *call on.* Can you figure out why some of these sentences are OK but others are wrong? What is the grammar rule for these verbs? Discuss this question with classmates. Write your answer here.

_____

_____

_____

[Check p. 31 for the answer. Do this only after you have discussed this with a classmate.]

The Grammar of Phrasal Verbs

A phrasal verb consists of a verb followed by a particle (or a preposition or an adverb) such as **after, away, back, over, in, into, out, on, off, up,** or **down.**

> *example:*   He didn't **turn off** the light.

In this sentence, the word **turn** is not enough to express the meaning of the sentence. It is necessary to have both **turn** and **off.** In addition, the meaning of **turn off** is not equal to the meaning of **turn** plus the meaning of **off. Turn off** is a phrasal verb.

Other common examples of phrasal verbs are **call up, put on, call on,** and **look after.**

Phrasal verbs cause a special problem for students of English grammar. In the Discover Grammar activity at the beginning of this unit, you saw that some phrasal verbs can be separated and some cannot when there is a noun object. In addition, some phrasal verbs must be separated when there is a pronoun object.

Group 1. Separable Phrasal Verbs

The phrasal verbs in this group can be separated when there is a noun object. For example, you can say, "call up Mike" or "call Mike up." If there is a pronoun object, the phrasal verb must be separated. For example, you have to say, "call him up," never "call up him."

Note that many of these expressions have more than one meaning. For example, **take off** means (1) to remove something, such as clothing, as well as (2) to leave the ground, such as an airplane or a rocket. Only the most common meanings are included here for the purposes of this grammar lesson. Read the examples to help you remember the meanings. As you read, practice the separation patterns for noun object and pronoun objects.

	No. 1 **VERB +** **NOUN**	No. 2 *Separated* *by Noun*	No. 3 **VERB +** **PRONOUN**	No. 4 *Separated* *by Pronoun*
call back (return a call)	**call back** John	**call** John **back**	—	**call** him **back**
call off (cancel)	**call off** the game	**call** the game **off**	—	**call** it **off**
call up (telephone)	**call up** the teacher	**call** the teacher **up**	—	**call** her **up**
cross out (draw a line through)	**cross out** the mistake	**cross** the mistake **out**	—	**cross** it **out**
figure out (find the answer to a problem)	**figure out** the answer	**figure** the answer **out**	—	**figure** it **out**
fill in (write information)	**fill in** the blank	**fill** the blank **in**	—	**fill** it **in**
fill out (complete a paper)	**fill out** the form	**fill** the form **out**	—	**fill** it **out**
find out (get information about something)	**find out** the price	**find** the price **out**	—	**find** it **out**
give away (give something to someone because you don't want it any longer)	**give away** the prize	**give** the prize **away**	—	**give** it **away**
give back (return something to someone)	**give back** the reward	**give** the reward **back**	—	**give** it **back**
hand in (submit)	**hand in** my paper	**hand** my paper **in**	—	**hand** it **in**
hand out (give one to everyone)	**hand out** the papers	**hand** the papers **out**	—	**hand** them **out**
leave out (omit)	**leave out** the butter	**leave** the butter **out**	—	**leave** it **out**

look up (look for information in a dictionary, the computer, etc.)	**look up** this word	**look** this word **up**	—	**look** it **up**
make up (invent a story)	**make up** a story	**make** a story **up**	—	**make** one **up**
pick up (1. lift; 2. go get someone)	**pick up** my son	**pick** my son **up**	—	**pick** him **up**
put away (return to the correct place)	**put away** the clothes	**put** the clothes **away**	—	**put** them **away**
put back (return to the original place)	**put back** the boxes	**put** the boxes **back**	—	**put** them **back**
put off (postpone)	**put off** the test	**put** the test **off**	—	**put** it **off**
put on (wear)	**put on** your coat	**put** your coat **on**	—	**put** it **on**
put out (extinguish)	**put out** the fire	**put** the fire **out**	—	**put** it **out**
take off (remove)	**take off** your shoes	**take** your shoes **off**	—	**take** them **off**
tear up (break into small pieces)	**tear up** the bill	**tear** the bill **up**	—	**tear** it **up**
throw away (discard, put in the trash)	**throw away** the bag	**throw** the bag **away**	—	**throw** it **away**
try on (check to see if clothing fits)	**try on** those shoes	**try** those shoes **on**	—	**try** them **on**
turn down (lower the volume)	**turn down** the radio	**turn** the radio **down**	—	**turn** it **down**
turn on (start)	**turn on** the lights	**turn** the lights **on**	—	**turn** them **on**
turn off (stop)	**turn off** the stereo	**turn** the stereo **off**	—	**turn** it **off**
turn up (increase the volume)	**turn up** the volume	**turn** the volume **up**	—	**turn** it **up**
wake up (stop sleeping)	**wake up** the baby	**wake** the baby **up**	—	**wake** him **up**

write down (make a note of something)	**write down** the name	**write** the name **down**	—	**write** it **down**

SUMMARY: The phrasal verbs in group 1 have **three** possible grammatical forms.

I called up John.   phrasal verb plus noun object (no. 1),
I called John up.   phrasal verb separated by noun object (no. 2),
I called him up.   phrasal verb separated by pronoun object (no. 4).

It is important to remember that you cannot say, "I called up him" (no. 3).

Exercise 1.   Vocabulary Practice (half of the group 1 verbs). Match the phrasal verb on the left with its meaning on the right by writing the letter of the meaning on the line by the number.

Phrasal Verb   *Meaning*

_____ 1. He <u>called</u> me <u>back</u>.   A. got information about

_____ 2. He <u>called off</u> the meeting.   B. started (some kind of machine)

_____ 3. She <u>crossed</u> her answer <u>out</u>.   C. found the answer to a problem

_____ 4. She <u>found out</u> the price.   D. took with my hand

_____ 5. I <u>filled out</u> the form.   E. returned to the original place

_____ 6. They <u>handed</u> their papers <u>in</u>.   F. checked to see if they fit

_____ 7. I <u>picked up</u> the coin.   G. returned a telephone call

_____ 8. We <u>put</u> the boxes <u>back</u>.   H. wrote the information on

_____ 9. I <u>tried on</u> the shirts.   I. submitted, gave

_____ 10. We finally <u>figured</u> it <u>out</u>.   J. drew a line through it

_____ 11. I <u>took off</u> my shoes.   K. omitted, did not include

_____ 12. I <u>gave</u> it <u>away</u>.   L. removed

_____ 13. I <u>made</u> the story <u>up</u>.   M. not do now, do later

_____ 14. We <u>left out</u> number 8.   N. invented

_____ 15. She <u>turned</u> it <u>on</u>.   O. canceled

_____ 16. I want to <u>put</u> it <u>off</u>.   P. give to someone because you don't want it now

Exercise 2. Vocabulary Practice (the other half of the group 1 verbs). Match the phrasal verb on the left with its meaning on the right by writing the letter of the meaning on the line by the number.

Phrasal Verb	*Meaning*
_____ 1. He <u>called</u> me <u>up</u>.	A. return to the correct place
_____ 2. I <u>filled in</u> the blanks.	B. go get
_____ 3. She <u>gave</u> the wallet <u>back</u>.	C. postpone
_____ 4. I <u>handed</u> them <u>out</u>.	D. stopped (a machine)
_____ 5. She <u>looked</u> the word <u>up</u>.	E. extinguished (a fire)
_____ 6. Can you <u>pick</u> me <u>up</u> after work?	F. wore
_____ 7. Please <u>put</u> the milk <u>away</u>.	G. contacted by telephone
_____ 8. We had to <u>put off</u> the game.	H. returned to someone
_____ 9. He <u>put</u> his coat <u>on</u>.	I. completed, entered the information
_____ 10. They <u>put</u> it <u>out</u> right away.	J. discard, put in the trash
_____ 11. She <u>tore</u> it <u>up</u> immediately.	K. made a note
_____ 12. Did you <u>throw away</u> the bag?	L. increased the volume
_____ 13. Please <u>turn</u> the radio <u>down</u>.	M. looked for information about
_____ 14. She <u>turned</u> it <u>off</u>.	N. broke into small pieces
_____ 15. I <u>turned up</u> the TV.	O. distributed to everyone
_____ 16. I <u>wrote</u> it <u>down</u>.	P. lower the volume

Exercise 3. Vocabulary Practice. Add the correct word to complete these sentences using phrasal verbs. Follow the examples.

1. *Ann:* Could I use your phone? I need to call ___up___ the bank. I lost my bank card.

   Sue: Of course you can. Here's the phone book so you can look the number ___up___.

   Ann: Thanks. I thought I put the card _____ in my wallet after I last used it, but it's not there now. I'm really worried.

2. *Bob:*   Let's watch the news. I want to find _____ who won the football game

today.

Amy: OK. Turn the TV _____. Let's watch Channel 7's news.

Bob: That sounds good. Hey, could you turn it _____ a little? I can't hear it.

Amy: The control is broken, so I can't turn it _____ any more. That's the

loudest it will go.

3. *Teacher:*   Class, I'm afraid we will not have a test today. I'd like to put it _____

until tomorrow.

Student: OK, but what about our homework?

Teacher: Right. Would everyone please hand _____ the assignment now? Just

pass your papers to the front of the room. And do it quickly, please.

Student: So do we have homework for tomorrow now that we have a test to study

for?

Teacher: I assume you have already studied for the test because it was supposed to

be today. The homework for tomorrow is to read pages 300 to 318 and

answer the questions on page 319. OK, everyone, write this _____.

Pages 300 to 318 and then the questions on page 319.

4. *Joe:*   Excuse me. I'd like to fill _____ a job application.

Clerk: OK, here is the form.

Joe: What should I write in this area?

Clerk: Don't fill _____ that area. It's clearly marked "For Office Use Only."

Joe: Question number 9 asks for the telephone number of my first boss, but I

don't know that number.

Clerk: Well, then, I guess you will have to leave that information _____.

Joe: Is it a problem if I do that?

Clerk: No, not really. I don't think anyone is going to call him _____ anyway.

Exercise 4.   Write the expression again using a pronoun object.

1. Look up the new words.   _____Look them up._____

2. She called John back.   _____

3. Please write down this number. _____

4. She tore up the letter.   _____

5. Don't turn the TV on now.   _____

6. He handed out the exams.   _____

7. I left out two questions.   _____

8. Did you fill out the form?   _____

9. Why did you leave Mary out?   _____

10. She called off the wedding.   _____

Group 2. Nonseparable Phrasal Verbs

The phrasal verbs in group 2 only have two patterns: verb plus noun object (no. 1) and verb plus object pronoun (no. 3). In other words, the verb and the particle are always together and the noun (or pronoun) comes afterward. These verbs are never separated by any object, whether it is a noun or a pronoun.

Some of the verbs in this group have three words. Three-word phrasal verbs are always nonseparable. For example, "The car ran out of gas" is correct, but "The car ran out gas of" is wrong. Some students find this group much easier than the first group because the word order is the regular English word order of subject-verb-object.

	No. 1 **VERB +** **NOUN**	**No. 2** *Separated* *by Noun*	**No. 3** **VERB +** **PRONOUN**	**No. 4** *Separated* *by Pronoun*
call on (ask a question in class)	**call on** the student	—	**call on** him	—
catch up (with) (reach the same level or position as)	**catch up with** the others	—	**catch up with** them	—
check in, into (register at a hotel)	**check into** the hotel	—	**check into** it	—
come across (find by chance)	**come across** a wallet	—	**come across** it	—
count on (depend on)	**count on** your help	—	**count on** it	—

get along (with) (be friends with)	**get along with** someone	—	**get along with** him	—
get in (enter)	**get in** a car	—	**get in** it	—
get off (exit)	**get off** a bus	—	**get off** it	—
get on (enter)	**get on** a plane	—	**get on** it	—
get out of (exit)	**get out of** a taxi	—	**get out of** it	—
get over (recover from an illness or a problem)	**get over** a cold	—	**get over** it	—
get through (complete)	**get through** the exam	—	**get through** it	—
go over (review or check carefully)	**go over** the test	—	**go over** it	—
look after (take care of)	**look after** the baby	—	**look after** him	—
look out (for) (be careful)	**look out for** that car!	—	**look out for** it	—
put up with (tolerate, stand)	**put up with** that noise	—	**put up with** it	—
run into (meet by chance)	**run into** an old friend	—	**run into** her	—
run out (of) (not have any more)	**run out of** gas	—	**run out of** it	—
watch out (for) (be careful)	**watch out for** that dog	—	**watch out for** it	—

SUMMARY: The phrasal verbs in group 2 have **two** possible grammatical forms.

The teacher went over the notes. I get along with John.	=	phrasal verb plus noun object (no. 1)

The teacher went over them. I get along with him.	=	phrasal verb plus pronoun object (no. 3)

It is important to remember that you *cannot* say, "The teacher went the notes over" or "The teacher went them over." In addition, you *cannot* say, "I get along Tom with" (no. 2) or "I get him along" (no. 4).

Exercise 5.   Fill in the blanks with the missing words of the phrasal verbs.

1. When I get _____ work every day, I get _____ my car and drive straight home.

2. When I was driving home yesterday, my car ran _____ _____ gas. I got _____ _____ my car and walked to a gas station to get some gasoline.

3. Every time Mrs. Jenks calls _____ Billy, he is asleep. I don't know how she puts _____ _____ him.

4. I've been absent for over a week, and now I have to work extra hard to catch _____ _____ my classmates. I've done some extra work that the teacher is going to go _____ after class today. I'm counting _____ her help to help me catch up.

5. My mom got _____ a plane to Seattle last night to go look _____ my grandmother. She had a heart attack and is in the hospital. My mom has checked _____ a hotel just across the street from the hospital. She's going to stay there till my grandmother gets better.

6. Mike, look _____ _____ that car!

Exercise 6.   Write the expression again using a pronoun object.

1. We ran out of sugar.   _____ We ran out of it. _____

2. She put up with Sue and Jamie.   _____

3. They're counting on Paul and me.   _____

4. I came across some old photos.   _____

5. The teacher went over the exam.   _____

6. I couldn't catch up with the students. _____

7. The professor called on Jim.   _____

8. I'm looking after my grandfather.   _____

9. We ran into Alan and Paul.   _____

10. Before my presentation, I went over my notes.   _____

Group 3. Phrasal Verbs without Objects

There are some phrasal verbs that do not usually have an object.★ Verbs in this group consist of the verb and a particle. Together they express a meaning; no object is usually possible. For example, **pass away** means to die. It is possible to say, "Mrs. Riley passed away," but it is not possible to say, "Mrs. Riley passed away her" or "Mrs. Riley passed her away."

Phrasal Verb (no object)

break down	(stop working)	My car **broke down.**
break up	(end a relationship)	Jack and Chris **broke up.**
catch on	(begin to understand)	It took me a long time to **catch on.**
come on	(hurry up)	**Come on!** We're going to be late.
eat out	(eat at a restaurant)	It's expensive to **eat out** every day.
get up	(leave bed)	What time do you usually **get up?**
give up	(stop trying)	I tried to learn French, but I **gave up.**
go off	(make a noise)	My alarm **went off** at 6:30.
grow up	(become an adult)	I **grew up** in Canada.
hold on	(wait)	**Hold on** a minute.
hurry up	(go faster)	**Hurry up** or we'll be late.
keep on	(continue)	She **kept on** talking.
show up	(arrive, appear at a place)	Not many people **showed up.**
slow down	(go more slowly)	Please **slow down.**
take off	(leave the ground)	The plane didn't **take off** on time.
wake up	(stop sleeping)	I **woke up** when you turned on the TV.

★Verbs that cannot have an object are called **intransitive verbs.** In most dictionaries, this will be coded as **vi** (verb intransitive).

Exercise 7. Read the meaning of the phrasal verb and then fill in the blank with the missing word.

	Phrasal Verb		*Meaning*
1. break	___up___	=	end a relationship
2. catch	_____	=	begin to understand
3. keep	_____	=	continue
4. break	_____	=	stop working
5. eat	_____	=	eat at a restaurant
6. come	_____	=	hurry up
7. give	_____	=	stop trying

8. take	_____	=	leave the ground
9. hurry	_____	=	go faster
10. get	_____	=	leave bed
11. show	_____	=	arrive, appear at a place
12. grow	_____	=	become an adult
13. wake	_____	=	stop sleeping
14. go	_____	=	make a noise
15. hold	_____	=	wait
16. slow	_____	=	go more slowly

Exercise 8.   Fill in each blank with the correct word to complete the sentence. Follow the example.

1. *Ann:*   Paula, slow ____*down*____! You're driving too fast!

   Paula: A few minutes ago you told me to hurry _____. Make up your mind!

2. *Vicky:*   Why were you late for work this morning?

   Fran: I set my alarm clock for 7 A.M. and at 7 A.M. it went _____, but I didn't feel like getting _____, so I kept _____ sleeping.

3. *Tim:*   Tony, come _____! We're going to be late, and you know Karen and Rachel are going to be really mad if we're late again.

   Tony: I'm trying. You know I hate eating _____ with Karen and Rachel. They have to do everything by the clock! It's just not fun. Why did you tell them that we would have dinner with them?

   Tim: Hold _____, Tony. You were the one who talked to them, not me.

4. *Beth:*   How was your flight?

   Pam: As soon as the plane took _____, I fell asleep. I didn't wake _____ until we were just about to land here.

Beth: You were able to sleep on the plane? I wish I could sleep on planes. I used

to try to do that, but I gave _____ a long time ago. It seems there is

almost always a crying baby near me on every flight.

5. *Carl:*   Jimmy, what do you want to be when you grow _____?

Jimmy: I want to be a mechanic so I can fix our car when it breaks _____.

6. *Ben:*   I'm glad that you and Irene could come to the party.

Kim: I'm sorry we didn't get here earlier. Irene was supposed to be at my place

at 6, but she didn't show _____ till 6:45.

Ben: Irene is always late. I used to expect her to come on time, too, but after she

was late a couple of times, I caught _____ and started subtracting

thirty minutes from the time I really wanted to meet. That way there were

no time problems.

Exercise 9.   Editing. Seven of the sentences contain an error connected to the grammar in this unit. Find the errors and correct them. Write C in front of the three sentences that are correct.

1. The teacher handed out the exams at 9 o'clock, and the students handed in them at 9:50.

2. We didn't look all the new words up when we were reading.

3. Jan is a dependable person, and I'm counting her on to make sure I arrive at the airport on time.

4. He didn't want the magazines, so he gave away them because he didn't want to throw them away.

5. Where did you come this article across? It's excellent!

6. The other students are ahead of me. I'll never catch them up.

7. When I was driving to school yesterday, my car broke it down.

8. We didn't need the batteries, so Karl threw it out.

9. Before Joanna buys a dress, she always tries it on.

10. I was born in Texas, but I grew up in England.

Speaking Activity

Exercise 10a.   Speaking Activity: Crossword Puzzle, Student A

Two students work together. Use the clues on this page to fill in as many of the words as possible. Then take turns asking each other questions about the information that is missing from the puzzle. Student A works on the first crossword puzzle while student B works on the second crossword puzzle. Do NOT look at your partner's puzzle at any time.

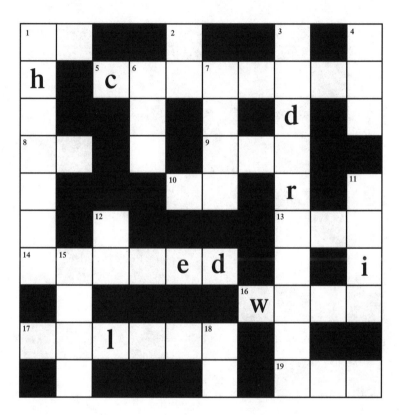

Across

5. What does "keep on doing something" mean?
8. My car ran out ____ gas.
13. If you figure out the problem "2 + 3," then you figured out the ___.
14. The first four letters are a part of your body. (*Hint:* The place where your fingers are.)
16. What does "hold on a minute" mean?
17. When teachers do this action (a phrasal verb), some students get nervous.
19. What does "pass away" mean?

Down

1. If you want to see your friend after work, you might ask, "When will you get ____ with work?"
2. The opposite of "turn off the lights" is to turn them ___.
6. What is the second word of the phrasal verb that means to eat in a restaurant?
18. Is it correct to say, "I polished all my shoes, and then I put away them"?

**Speaking
Activity**

Exercise 10b.   Speaking Activity: Crossword Puzzle, Student B

Two students work together. Use the clues on this page to fill in as many of the words as possible. Then take turns asking each other questions about the information that is missing from the puzzle. Student B works on the second crossword puzzle while student A works on the first crossword puzzle. Do NOT look at your partner's puzzle at any time!

Across

1. We handed the papers in ___ the teacher.
9. a form of the verb *to be*
10. The last two letters of the phrasal verb that means to take care of someone
14. Yesterday there was a test. What did the teacher do at the beginning of the class? She ___ out the exams.
17. What phrasal verb means the action that teachers might do to students in class?

Down

3. What does "catch on" to something mean?
4. Is it correct to say, "I wrote it down"?
7. If you don't want anyone to read your secret letter, you might ___ it up.
11. What does "leave out" mean?
12. To enter a taxi is to get ___ the taxi.
15. If the toys are in their correct, usual place, this means that you put them ___.

Exercise 11.   Multiple Choice. Circle the letter of the correct answer.

1. "Did you give the teacher your essay?"

   "Yes, I _____ a few minutes ago."

   (A) handed in it   (C) turned it down

   (B) handed it in   (D) turned down it

2. "How is Janice?"

   "She's better now. It took her a long time to _____."

   (A) get over the flu   (C) get the flu over

   (B) get over them   (D) get them over

3. "How did you find _____ about the test scores?"

   "I e-mailed the teacher."

   (A) back   (C) up

   (B) in   (D) out

4. "Why did the plane crash?"

   "Investigators believe that a bomb went _____ during the flight."

   (A) on   (C) in

   (B) off   (D) out

5. "Your English is really good."

   "Thanks, but it took me many years to be able to catch _____ to American pronun-

   ciation."

   (A) up   (C) on

   (B) off   (D) with

6. "Did you complete the form?"

   "Yes, I filled _____ before I left the office yesterday. Here it is."

   (A) it out   (C) out it

   (B) them out   (D) out them

7. They had to call the game off because _____.

   (A) the weather was bad   (C) the tickets were not colorful

   (B) the ball was round   (D) the players were in good condition

8. Which one of these is correct?

   (A) I counted him on.   (C) I looked up them.

   (B) I called him on.   (D) I looked after them.

Exercise 12.   Review Test

Part 1.   Fill in the blanks with the missing words.

1. I was so tired when I finally got home. I got _____ of my car and went in my

   house. I put a pizza in the oven and set the alarm for sixteen minutes. Then I sat on

   the sofa to watch the news. I used the remote control to turn _____ the TV. I

   couldn't hear it very well, so I turned _____ the sound. A few minutes later, the

   oven clock went _____, so I turned _____ the oven and put the pizza on

   a large plate. I was so hungry that I ate the whole pizza. When I got _____ from

   the sofa, I turned the lights _____ and went to bed.

2. In 1997, I went to New York City. I saw a lot of interesting things there, but the thing

   that I will never forget was the taxi ride from the airport to my hotel. I asked the

   driver how much it would cost to get from the airport to my hotel, but he just kept

   saying, "Get _____, please. Please get _____." When we left the airport, I

   couldn't believe how fast he was driving. I asked him to slow _____, but he

   kept _____ driving fast. I tried several times to make him drive more slowly, but

   I finally gave _____ because he wasn't paying attention to me or my questions. I

   hope that I never run _____ another taxi driver like that one again.

Part 2.   Read each sentence carefully. Look at the underlined part. If the under-
            lined part is correct, circle the word *correct*. If it is wrong, circle the wrong
            part and write the correct form above.

correct   wrong   1. *Anna:*   Did you finish all the work?

                        Bob: Yes, I <u>got it through</u> at noon.

correct   wrong   2. What time did your plane finally <u>take it off</u>?

correct   wrong   3. I called the police when I couldn't <u>put up with</u> that noise any

                       more.

correct   wrong   4. *Sam:*   Betty is a great friend.

Anna: Yes, I agree. You can always <u>count her on</u>.

correct   wrong   5. *Dan:*   Where are those old tennis shoes?

Tim: I <u>threw them away</u> last week. They were really old.

correct   wrong   6. *Rick:*   Is that a true story?

Wes: No, I <u>made it up</u>.

correct   wrong   7. *Anna:*   Why didn't you answer numbers 5 and 6?

Sam: I <u>left out them</u> because I didn't understand them.

correct   wrong   8. *Meg:*   Some friends just heard that there won't be a baseball

game today.

Zeke: That's right. We're <u>putting them off</u> until next Monday.

Extra Writing Practice

Situation: You flew from your city to London. Your friend Henry said he would take you to the airport. Your flight left at 9 A.M., and Henry promised to be at your house at 7 A.M. at the latest. Because Henry was still not at your house at 7:30 A.M., you were worried and called his house. He was not there, so you called your good friend Paul even though it was really early in the morning. Paul gladly helped you. He came to your house in his car and took you to the airport. Because of Paul, your trip to London was successful. You are in London now. Write a letter to Henry in which you are angry for what happened. Tell him that Paul helped you.

Be sure to practice as many phrasal verbs as you can. For example, you might say, "You said you would take me to the airport, but at the last minute, I had to <u>call</u> Paul <u>up</u>." Always underline the grammar point that you have used so the teacher can see what you are trying to practice.

Answers to DISCOVER GRAMMAR on pages 14–15:

Phrasal verbs consist of a verb and a particle. The examples here are *call up, turn on,* and *call on.* With some phrasal verbs, you can separate the verb and the particle with an object: <u>*call up* the man, *call* the man *up.*</u> When there is a pronoun object, the phrasal verb must be separated: <u>*call him up*</u> (but not <u>*call up* him</u>). With other phrasal verbs, you can never separate the verb and the particle: <u>*call on* the student</u> (but not <u>*call* the student *on*</u>) and <u>*call on* him</u> (but not <u>*call* him *on*</u>). Every time you learn a phrasal verb, you need to learn whether or not it is separable.

Unit 3

Past Progressive Tense

1. form: *be* + PRESENT PARTICIPLE
2. affirmative
3. negative
4. questions
5. usage; contrast with simple past tense
6. *when* vs. *while*

**When Scott arrived at 8:30, Mark WAS STUDYING at his desk.
Scott didn't stay very long because Mark WAS STUDYING.**

Discover Grammar

1. Look at the sentences below. Some of them are correct, and some of them are wrong. Read the sentences and try to understand the grammar rule for these sentences.
2. Work with a partner. Discuss your ideas.

Situation A. It started to rain at 5 A.M. I woke up at 7 A.M. The rain finally stopped at 8 A.M.
  1. When I woke up, it was raining. (correct)
  2. When I woke up, it rained. (wrong)

Situation B. Tom was angry. He got in his car and started to drive very fast. Unfortunately, his car hit another car. It was a big accident.

3. When Tom had the accident, he drove very fast. (wrong)

4. When Tom had the accident, he was driving very fast. (correct)

Situation C. Jim decided to drive his car to New York. On the way, there was a problem with one of the tires.

5. While he was driving to New York, he had a flat tire. (correct)

6. While he was driving to New York, he was having a flat tire. (wrong)

Situation D. Jim had a car accident. He called the police.

7. When Jim had a car accident, he called the police. (correct)

8. When Jim had a car accident, he was calling the police. (wrong)

Situation E. Irene started cooking dinner at 3:30. At 6:15, the main course was finally finished. Irene was tired. She picked up a plate from the table to put it back in the cabinet. She dropped it, and it broke into many pieces.

9. She was putting away the plate when she dropped it. (correct)

10. She was putting away the plate while she dropped it. (wrong)

Situation F. A lot of people were in the room. In fact, all the chairs were taken. The president entered the room. Everyone stood up.

11. When the president entered the room, everyone stood up. (correct)

12. While the president was entering the room, everyone stood up. (strange)

13. When the president entered the room, everyone was standing up. (false)

What is the grammar rule for this unit? Write your answers to these questions and then discuss them with a partner or in small groups.

1. When do you use *when* and *while?* _____

_____

_____

2. Sometimes the verb is past tense and sometimes the verb has *was* or *were* and VERB + -*ing.* When do we use each of these? _____

_____

_____

[Check p. 44 for the answers.]

Past Progressive Tense of Verbs

Simple Past	*Past Progressive*
I **walked** to school yesterday.	While I **was walking** to school yesterday, my homework fell out of my book.
Did you **drive** to Miami yesterday?	Did you fall asleep while you **were driving** to Miami yesterday?
He **made** a sandwich.	He **was making** a sandwich when he cut himself.
She **wrote** a letter.	She **was writing** a letter when the phone rang.
We **played** baseball.	While we **were playing** baseball, it started to rain.

1. Past progressive tense has two parts: **was/were** and **VERB + –ing.**
    examples: I was eating, they were playing, he was running

2. Use past progressive tense for an action that was happening when another action interrupted it. In other words, the first action began and was continuing when the second action occurred. Use past continuous for the first or longer action and use simple past for the second action (i.e., the one that interrupts the first).

    > *examples:*　I was eating dinner when the telephone rang.
    > The rain started while we were playing baseball.

3. In general, we use **when** with shorter actions and **while** with longer actions.

    > *examples:*　When the rain began, we were playing baseball.
    > While we were playing baseball, the rain began.

4. The rules for making negative or making a question are the regular rules for the verb *be*. To make a negative, you can add **not** or you can make a contraction (**wasn't** or **weren't**). To make a question, put **was** or **were** in front of the subject.

    > *examples:*　Were you sleeping when the fire started? What were you doing?
    > I wasn't doing anything when you called. I wasn't busy at all.

5. It is possible to use **when** with two past tense verbs. In this case, it means that the **when** clause action happened first and then the second action happened.

    > *examples:*　When he sat down, the chair broke.
    > When the plane stopped at the gate, everyone stood up.

6. It is possible to use **while** with two past progressive tense verbs. In this case, it means that both actions were happening at the same time.

> *examples:*   While she was eating, I was watching TV.
> While I was doing my homework, my brother was playing tennis.

7. The **when** clause and the **while** clause can be before the main clause or after it. Both orders are possible.

> *examples:*   When she called, I was watching TV. OR I was watching TV when she called.
> While I was studying, I fell asleep. OR I fell asleep while I was studying.

Note: A **clause** is a group of words with a subject and a verb. Every sentence has at least one clause. Study these sentences that have been divided into clauses.

a. Matt can play the guitar, | and | Rae can sing. (2 clauses)
b. They failed the test | because they didn't study enough. (2)
c. Kevin woke up | when he heard the noise. (2)
d. While she was walking up the steps, | she dropped her papers. (2)
e. She wants to return the radio | that she bought yesterday | because it doesn't work well. (3)

NOTE TO ADVANCED STUDENTS

There are two kinds of clauses: **independent clauses,** which can stand on their own and be understood; and **dependent clauses** which cannot stand on their own and depend on information in another clause to be understood.

In example *a* above, both of the clauses are independent. The word **and** is a connector. However, in examples *b* and *c*, the first clause is independent, and the second is dependent. In example *d,* the first clause is dependent, and the second is independent. In example *e,* there is one independent clause followed by two dependent clauses.

Can you write a sentence that has only one independent clause? This is not so difficult. There are many sentences like this.

How about a sentence that has only one dependent clause? This is impossible. This is a common error that some learners make. Here are some wrong examples and corrections.

wrong: Because I studied very hard.
correct: I passed the test because I studied very hard. OR
correct: Because I studied very hard, I passed the test.

CAREFUL! Do not make these common mistakes.

1. Do not use **was/were** and a verb without **–ing**.
    wrong: When I got my first job, I was live in Los Angeles.
    correct: When I got my first job, I was living in Los Angeles.

2. Don't mix up past progressive tense and simple past tense.
    wrong: We played tennis when the rain began.
    correct: We were playing tennis when the rain began.

    wrong: I cut the onions. Then I was putting them in the soup.
    correct: I cut the onions. Then I put them in the soup.

3. Don't use **did** in a question with past progressive.
    wrong: Did you were watching TV when she called you?
    correct: Were you watching TV when she called you?

Exercise 1.   Write these verbs in simple past and past progressive tenses.
Follow the examples.

	Simple Past	*Past Progressive*
1. I eat	I ate	I was eating
2. he does		
3. they ask		
4. she takes		
5. we watch		
6. it gets		
7. I make		
8. he begins		

Exercise 2.   Underline the correct answer. Follow the example.

1. Jill came to my house last night. It was 6:30. I (made, <u>was making</u>) dinner when she
    (<u>arrived</u>, was arriving). She didn't stay at my house for a long time. She only (<u>stopped</u>,
    was stopping) to say hello. After about ten or fifteen minutes, Jill (<u>left</u>, was leaving).

2. Many Americans can remember exactly what they (did, were doing) when they heard the news about President Kennedy's assassination. I can recall that exact minute. I (attended, was attending) a meeting.

3. While I (listened, was listening) to the teacher's lecture, I heard two words that I (didn't know, wasn't knowing). I (wrote, was writing) down the words, and later I asked my friend what they meant.

4. Paul and I have a test tomorrow, so this afternoon we studied together. We (met, were meeting) at the library. We studied for about two hours. Then we (got, were getting) something to eat. After that, I (went, was going) home, but Paul returned to the library to study some more. While I (went, was going) home, I decided to go to the bank to get some cash. After that, I went home.

5. Last Sunday was a very important day for our baseball team. We had our last game of the season. The game (started, was starting) at 1 P.M. All of the players from both teams (went, were going) on the field. After we (warmed, were warming) up, the game (began, was beginning). Everyone (enjoyed, was enjoying) the game when it suddenly began to rain.

Exercise 3.   Read each sentence and decide whether the correct tense for the verb in parentheses should be simple past or past progressive. Write the correct form of the verb in each sentence. Follow the example.

example: (write) (**A**) He _____wrote_____ six letters last night.

(**B**) He _____was writing_____ a letter when I called.

(**C**) How many letters _____did_____ he _____write_____ to his sister?

(read)   1. After I ate breakfast, I _____ the newspaper.

2. While my wife _____ the newspaper, I was watching TV.

3. At the time of the earthquake, I _____ a magazine.

(study   4. Rachel was busy when I called. She _____ math.

5. Rachel _____ math for an hour every day last week.

6. Rachel watched a TV show, and then she _____ math.

(play)   7. Mark and I _____ tennis after school.

8. Mark and I _____ tennis when he fell and hurt his arm.

9. _____ Mark _____ tennis with you when he fell and hurt his arm?

(have)   10. The party was very successful. Everyone _____ a great time.

11. While everyone _____ a great time at the party, I was at the library because I had to finish a big report for my history class.

12. *A:* How was the party? _____ you _____ a good time?

B: It was great. I _____ a wonderful time there!

Exercise 4.   Read the list of words. Then read the miniparagraph below. Write the list of words as a single sentence with the correct verb tenses so that it fits well into the miniparagraph. Follow the example.

1. While / we / play tennis, / it / begin / to rain.
   Michael and I met at the tennis courts at noon yesterday. ___*While we were*___ ___*playing tennis, it began to rain.*___ Of course we had to stop playing. When the rain finally stopped, we couldn't play because the courts were too wet.

2. While / he / talk on the phone, / I / cut up the onions.
   Luke wanted to cook vegetable soup. He took three onions from the refrigerator. Then he got a knife. He was ready to cut up the onions. Suddenly the phone rang._____
   _____ When Luke finished his call, he came back into the kitchen. He was surprised that all the onions were cut up.

3. When / I / wake up this morning, / it / rain.

My plans for today included cutting the grass and painting the garage. However,_____

_____

That's the reason I was able to watch TV all day instead of doing those two chores.

4. When / he / read the news, / he start / to cry.

Kamil spent ten months studying English. About a month ago, he took TOEFL★ for

the fourth time. His parents told Kamil that if he didn't pass this time, he would have

to return to his country right away. This afternoon Kamil got a letter from the testing

office. His face was very serious as he opened the letter. _____

_____ At first, I didn't know if he

was happy or sad, but then I could see that he was smiling, too. Kamil had finally

passed the test!

★TOEFL = Test of English as a Foreign Language; an exam to demonstrate English ability.

Speaking Activity

Exercise 5.   Speaking Activity. What were you doing at 2 P.M. yesterday?

Step 1.   Choose five of the times below. Write the times in any order on the short
           lines.
Step 2.   Work with a partner. Take turns asking each other the question, "What
           were you doing at (time) yesterday (OR yesterday morning OR yesterday
           afternoon OR last night)?
Step 3.   Write your partner's actions on the lines. Use your partner's name.

            example: Sammy was watching TV.

Times: 2:30 P.M.   6:00 A.M.   9:00 A.M.   6:30 P.M.
           10:15 A.M.   noon   11:00 P.M.   2:00 P.M.
           4:00 P.M.   7:30 A.M.   8:30 P.M.   11:15 A.M.

        Time   *Action*

1. _____   _____

2. _____   _____

3. _____   _____

4. _____   _____

5. _____   _____

Speaking Activity

Exercise 6.   Speaking Activity. And that's why Mr. Barron got angry

Situation: Mr. Barron was teaching math class. He had to go to the office to get a book. He told the students that he would be back in a few minutes, and he asked everyone to do the exercises on page 72. He also asked them to be quiet while he was gone. When Mr. Barron came back, he couldn't believe what the students were doing. He got so angry. He shouted, "Everyone, stop this now!"

Who was doing what? There are two groups of names and actions. Student A should do one group, and student B should do the other group. In each group, there are seven names or pairs of names and seven actions.

Step 1.   Work in your area only (A or B). Draw lines to connect the seven subjects and seven actions. Mix up the lines. You will make seven new sentences.

Now you have the pieces to make a sentence about the situation. For example, if student A draws a line from "Sammy" to "tell a joke," then your new sentence in the past progressive tense is "Sammy was telling a joke when Mr. Barron entered the room, and that's why Mr. Barron got angry." Remember, we are practicing past progressive tense.

Step 2.   Work with a partner. You will ask *yes-no* questions about your partner's sentences in order to guess his or her seven sentences. Student A will ask about B's sentences, and student B will ask about A's sentences. Every question must contain some phrase about Mr. Barron such as "when Mr. Barron entered the room," "when Mr. Barron got back," or "when Mr. Barron came in the room."

For example, student A can ask, "Was Susan standing near the window when Mr. Barron entered the room?" If student B has a line from "Susan" to "stand near the window," then B says, "Yes, Susan was standing near the window when Mr. Barron came in the room, and that's why he got angry." And it is still student A's turn to ask another question.

If student B does not have a line from "Susan" to "stand near the window," then B says, "No, Susan wasn't standing near the window when Mr. Barron got back. That's not correct." And it is student B's turn to ask a question.

The winner is the first student to guess all seven of his or her partner's sentences.

Student A

Sammy	talk to Mike
Maria	look out the window
Paul	read a comic book
Joe and Sue	do the exercise on page 72
Christina	tell a joke
Chang	write a letter
Julie	drawing a picture

Student B

Jonathan	sleep
Susan	stand near the window
Kirk	daydream about summer vacation
Tim and Bob	laugh very loudly
Shawn	stand on the teacher's desk
Pierre	do last night's homework
Mohamad	make animal noises

Exercise 7. Multiple Choice. Circle the letter of the correct answer.

1. "Hey, did you hear the thunder during the rainstorm this afternoon?"

   "No, I didn't. I _____ to some music, and I had the volume so loud that I didn't

   hear anything outside at all."

   (A) listened   (C) was listen

   (B) was listening   (D) listening

2. "What _____ last night?"

   "I went to see a movie, and then I did my history homework."

   (A) were you doing   (C) doing you

   (B) did you do   (D) did you

3. "Officer, what do you think caused the accident?"

   "I think your friend _____ the car too fast."

   (A) was drive   (C) drove

   (B) was drove   (D) was driving

4. *A:* Hey, I called your house last night, but no one was home.

   B: Oh, really? What time was it?

   A: About eight.

   B: You're right. I wasn't home then. At 8, I _____ my cousin.

   (A) visited   (C) was visiting

   (B) was visit   (D) visiting

5. First, I washed the car. After that, I _____ lunch.

   (A) cooked   (C) were cooking

   (B) was cooked   (D) was cooking

6. When you entered the room, who _____ at the table?

   (A) was sitting   (C) was sat

   (B) sat   (D) was sit

7. *Bob:*   This food is great.

   Julia: Thanks. It took me two hours to cook it.

   Bob: Wow, that's a long time. Did Sue help you?

   Julia: No, she couldn't.

   Bob: Why not?

   Julia: She was busy the whole time.

   Bob: What was she doing?

   Julia: Well, while I was cooking, she _____ her homework.

   (A) doing   (C) did

   (B) was doing   (D) was did

8. *Tom:*   Do you remember what you _____ when you heard the news that someone

           assassinated Kennedy?

   Ken: Yes, I do. I sat down in a chair and closed my eyes. I was so shocked that I

           couldn't talk for the next few minutes.

   (A) were doing   (C) did

   (B) was doing   (D) do

Exercise 8.   Review Test

Part 1.   Underline the correct words.

1. Washington was 57 years old when he (became, was becoming) the first president of the United States.

2. Shortly after his reelection, someone (shot, was shooting) Abraham Lincoln.

3. He (was putting, put) the bread in the oven. While it (baked, was baking), he made chicken soup. When he (finished, was finishing) the soup, we all ate dinner.

4. When the plane (was taking, took) off, there was a big problem, so the captain just drove the plane back to the gate. We had to wait until they fixed the plane. This took three hours. While we (waited, were waiting), the airline gave us free food and drinks.

5. When he (plugged, was plugging) the radio into the wall, the lights went out. (*Hint:* The first action caused the second.) My little brother was really afraid. He (watched, was watching) TV alone in his room.

Part 2.   Read each sentence carefully. Look at the underlined part. If the underlined part is correct, circle the word *correct*. If it is wrong, circle the wrong part and write the correct form above.

correct   wrong   1. I <u>hurt</u> my hand yesterday while I was playing tennis.

correct   wrong   2. <u>Did you watching</u> TV when she called?

correct   wrong   3. Last year I <u>was live</u> in Mexico City. After that, I moved to Houston.

correct   wrong   4. Bill and Sally say that they often get calls during meals. In fact, when I was there for dinner last night, someone called. When the telephone rang, we <u>were eating</u>. However, no one answered it. Bill and Sally told me that they never take calls during meals.

correct   wrong   5. Where were you when the accident <u>was happen</u>?

FOR MORE ADVANCED STUDENTS

In general, we use **when** with short actions and **while** with longer actions. However, it is almost always possible to use **when. While** can only be used when we think that the action took a longer amount of time.

examples: When I called Sam, he was eating dinner. (correct)
While I called Sam, he was eating dinner. (wrong; **while** cannot be used here)

While I was reading, I fell asleep. (correct)
When I was reading, I fell asleep. (correct; **when** can be used instead of **while**)

Extra Writing Practice

Situation: There was a robbery at the bank. Three people were in the bank and saw everything. You are the police officer who interviewed these three people after the robbery. Write your summary for each person.

Be sure to practice the grammar in this unit by telling what each person was doing when the robber came in, during the robbery, and when the police arrived. For example, you might write, "The old man <u>was waiting</u> in line when the robber came in the bank." Always underline the grammar point that you have used so the teacher can see what you are trying to practice.

Answers to DISCOVER GRAMMAR on pages 32–33:

1. In general, we use *when* with sudden actions and *while* with longer actions. 2. In general, we use simple past tense with short or sudden actions and *was/were* + VERB + *-ing* (past progressive) with longer actions. If one action is happening and a second action interrupts, we use past progressive with the longer action and past with the action that interrupts the first one.

Unit 4

Present Perfect Tense

1. form: *have/has* + PAST PARTICIPLE; question; negative
2. past participles
3. Usage No. 1: Recent past action that is important to now
4. Usage No. 2: Past experience, indefinite past time
5. Usage No. 3: Past action or situation that continues now
6. *since* vs. *for*
7. Usage No. 4: With *yet*
8. Usage No. 5: With a superlative
9. Usage No. 6: With *the first . . . , the third . . .*
10. Usage No. 7: Repetition of an action before now (exact time is not important)
11. Comparing simple past tense and present perfect tense

Yes, I'VE FLOWN on a 747 lots of times. I think the first time I FLEW on that kind of jet was when I WENT to India in 1996.

Have you *ever* FLOWN on a 747?

In this unit, you will learn about present perfect tense of verbs. Here are examples of the tenses that you already know and some examples of present perfect tense.

simple present tense	I **play** tennis every Saturday.	Jill **drives** to school.
simple past tense	I **played** tennis last Saturday.	Jill **drove** to school yesterday.
present progressive tense	I **am** not **playing** tennis now.	Jill **is driving** to school now.
be going to + VERB (future)	I **am going to play** tennis tomorrow.	Jill**'s** not **going to drive** to school tomorrow.
past progressive tense	I **was playing** tennis when it began to rain.	Jill **was driving** to school when she had an accident.
present perfect tense	I **have played** tennis for ten years.	Jill **has** never **driven** a BMW.

Present Perfect Tense

In the two examples above, you can see that present perfect tense consists of two parts: **have** or **has** and the **past participle.** In order to understand and use present perfect tense well, you need to know the past participle forms, so we will begin this unit with past participle forms. Learn them as quickly as you can so you can continue with the rest of the unit.

Past Participle

All verbs in English have three basic forms: present, past, and **past participle**.

The past and past participle forms of **REGULAR VERBS** use **-ed.** These two forms are the same. Examples are **work, worked, worked** and **study, studied, studied.**

Present	*Past*	*Past Participle*
play	played	**played**
work	worked	**worked**
react	reacted	**reacted**

The past and past participle forms of **IRREGULAR VERBS** are different. Common endings for the past participle forms of irregular verbs include **-en, -ne,** or **-n,** but there are many possibilities. Some irregular forms are the same for both past and past participle.

Present	*Past*	*Past Participle*
see	saw	**seen**
go	went	**gone**
wear	wore	**worn**

The good news for students is that only a small number of all the verbs in English are irregular. Students must memorize the irregular forms that are most commonly used.

60 Commonly Used Irregular Past and Past Participle Forms of Verbs*

Present	Past	Past Participle	Present	Past	Past Participle
1. be	was/were	been	31. leave	left	left
2. become	became	become	32. lend	lent	lent
3. begin	began	begun	33. let	let	let
4. break	broke	broken	34. lose	lost	lost
5. bring	brought	brought	35. make	made	made
6. build	built	built	36. meet	met	met
7. buy	bought	bought	37. put	put	put
8. catch	caught	caught	38. read	read	read
9. choose	chose	chosen	39. ride	rode	ridden
10. come	came	come	40. run	ran	run
11. cost	cost	cost	41. say	said	said
12. cut	cut	cut	42. see	saw	seen
13. drink	drank	drunk	43. sell	sold	sold
14. drive	drove	driven	44. send	sent	sent
15. do	did	done	45. show	showed	shown
16. eat	ate	eaten	46. sing	sang	sung
17. fall	fell	fallen	47. sit	sat	sat
18. feel	felt	felt	48. sleep	slept	slept
19. find	found	found	49. speak	spoke	spoken
20. fly	flew	flown	50. spend	spent	spent
21. forget	forgot	forgotten	51. steal	stole	stolen
22. freeze	froze	frozen	52. swim	swam	swum
23. get	got	gotten	53. take	took	taken
24. give	gave	given	54. teach	taught	taught
25. go	went	gone	55. tell	told	told
26. have	had	had	56. think	thought	thought
27. hit	hit	hit	57. understand	understood	understood
28. hold	held	held	58. wear	wore	worn
29. keep	kept	kept	59. win	won	won
30. know	knew	known	60. write	wrote	written

*For a longer list, see the Appendix on page 199.

Exercise 1.   Write the missing past participle forms.

	Present	Past	Past Participle		Present	Past	Past Participle
1.	be	was/were	_____	11.	lose	lost	_____
2.	make	made	_____	12.	see	saw	_____
3.	forget	forgot	_____	13.	freeze	froze	_____
4.	show	showed	_____	14.	sing	sang	_____
5.	sit	sat	_____	15.	sleep	slept	_____
6.	hit	hit	_____	16.	leave	left	_____
7.	steal	stole	_____	17.	swim	swam	_____
8.	take	took	_____	18.	teach	taught	_____
9.	tell	told	_____	19.	break	broke	_____
10.	think	thought	_____	20.	run	ran	_____

After you have checked and studied exercise 1, do Quiz 1, page 68.

Exercise 2.   Write the missing past participle forms.

	Present	Past	Past Participle		Present	Past	Past Participle
1.	say	said	_____	11.	choose	chose	_____
2.	wear	wore	_____	12.	win	won	_____
3.	write	wrote	_____	13.	become	became	_____
4.	begin	began	_____	14.	bring	brought	_____
5.	ride	rode	_____	15.	come	came	_____
6.	speak	spoke	_____	16.	spend	spent	_____
7.	buy	bought	_____	17.	put	put	_____
8.	catch	caught	_____	18.	meet	met	_____
9.	drink	drank	_____	19.	drive	drove	_____
10.	eat	ate	_____	20.	fall	fell	_____

After you have checked and studied exercise 2, do Quiz 2, page 68.

Exercise 3.   Write the missing past participle forms.

	Present	Past	Past Participle		Present	Past	Past Participle
1.	feel	felt	_____	11.	do	did	_____
2.	find	found	_____	12.	lend	lent	_____
3.	sell	sold	_____	13.	send	sent	_____
4.	hold	held	_____	14.	read	read	_____
5.	keep	kept	_____	15.	know	knew	_____
6.	cost	cost	_____	16.	cut	cut	_____
7.	let	let	_____	17.	fly	flew	_____
8.	get	got	_____	18.	give	gave	_____
9.	go	went	_____	19.	have	had	_____
10.	build	built	_____	20.	understand	understood	_____

After you have checked and studied exercise 3, do Quiz 3, page 69.

Exercise 4.   Extra Practice. Some people find it easier to learn the past participles in small groups according to pronunciation or spelling patterns. Write the past participles that belong in these groups. Follow the examples. (Some verbs may be used twice.)

1. long *i*   long *o*   *-en*

____drive____   ____drove____   ____driven____

_____   _____   _____

_____   _____   _____

2. present   *-aught*   *-aught*

____catch____   ____caught____   ____caught____

_____   _____   _____

3. All 3 forms are the same.

____cost____   ____cost____   ____cost____

_____   _____   _____

_____   _____   _____

_____   _____   _____

_____   _____   _____

4. present   past   present + *-en*

____eat____   ____ate____   ____eaten____

_____   _____   _____

_____   _____   _____

5. long *e*   long *o*   *-en*

____speak____   ____spoke____   ____spoken____

_____   _____   _____

_____   _____   _____

6. present   *-ought*   *-ought*

____bring____   ____brought____   ____brought____

_____   _____   _____

_____   _____   _____

_____   _____   _____

7. short *i*   short *a*   short *u*

__begin__   __began__   __begun__

_____   _____   _____

_____   _____   _____

8. present   past   same as present

__become__   __became__   __become__

_____   _____   _____

_____   _____   _____

9. present   past   present + -*n*

__drive__   __drove__   __driven__

_____   _____   _____

_____   _____   _____

_____   _____   _____

_____   _____   _____

Present Perfect Tense of Verbs

Present perfect tense consists of two parts: **have** (or **has**) + **PAST PARTICIPLE**. It is also possible to use a contraction: **'ve** for **have** and **'s** for **has.**

	work	**live**	**be**	**do**
I	I have worked	I've lived	I have been	I have done
you	you have worked	you have lived	you have been	you've done
he	he has worked	he's lived	he has been	he's done
she	she has worked	she has lived	she's been	she has done
it	it has worked	it has lived	it has been	it has done
we	we have worked	we have lived	we've been	we have done
they	they have worked	they have lived	they have been	they have done

Question

Making a question with present perfect tense is very easy. You put **have** or **has** before the subject.

He **has** gone to France.   **Has** he gone to France?

She **has** painted a picture.   What kind of picture **has** she painted?

They **have** all the work.   **Have** they done a good job?

Negative

Making a negative with present perfect tense is easy. You add the word **not** after **have** or **has**: **have not, has not**. It is also possible to use a contraction: **haven't** or **hasn't.** (Do not use **don't** or **doesn't.**)

I have lived here for two months.   I **haven't** lived here all my life.

Mrs. Wills has traveled to Egypt.   Mr. Will **has not** been outside the U.S.

Have you eaten at McDonalds?   **Haven't** you eaten at McDonalds?

CAREFUL! Watch out for these common mistakes.

India

1. Do not forget to use **have** or **has** with the past participle.
   wrong: I never gone to India.
   correct: I have never gone to India.

2. Do not use **have** or **has** with the wrong subject.
   wrong: Sarah have already finished all the homework.
   correct: Sarah has already finished all the homework.

3. Do not use **don't**, **doesn't**, or **didn't** in present perfect tense. Don't confuse **don't have** with **haven't**. Don't confuse **doesn't have** with **hasn't**.
   wrong: We don't have eaten at that restaurant yet.
   correct: We haven't eaten at that restaurant yet.

4. Do not use **do**, **does**, or **did** in question form of present perfect tense.
   wrong: How many countries did you visited in your life?
   correct: How many countries have you visited in your life?

Exercise 5. Write the correct forms of the verbs in the blanks. Follow the examples.

	go		*work*		*do*		*be*
I	have gone	you	_____	I	_____	he	_____
you	have gone	he	_____	you	_____	I	_____
they	have gone	I	_____	we	_____	you	_____
he	has gone	she	_____	he	_____	Jill	_____
Lim	has gone	it	_____	they	_____	Jill and I	_____

Exercise 6. Write the correct statement, negative, and question forms of present perfect. Practice contractions in the negative forms. Follow the examples.

	Affirmative	Negative	Question
1. he / go	he has gone	he hasn't gone	has he gone?
2. I / make	_____	_____	_____
3. they / speak	_____	_____	_____

4. you / put   _____ _____ _____

5. you / sing   _____ _____ _____

6. we / do   _____ _____ _____

7. she / think   _____ _____ _____

8. Ken / fly   _____ _____ _____

9. Zina / work   _____ _____ _____

10. I / write   _____ _____ _____

Speaking Activity

Exercise 7.   Speaking Activity

Step 1. Inside the parentheses below, write down ten verbs from the list on page 47.

Step 2. Write the correct present perfect form according to the subject (noun or pronoun).

Step 3. Work with a partner. Student A reads one verb and subject combination. Student B has to give the correct form.
A: "go, you"
B: "You have gone."
A: "That's correct." (Now B has to ask a question.)
B: "eat, the cats"
A: "The cats have eaten."

Step 4. If you want to make this exercise more useful, then try to make a more complicated sentence. For example, you could say "You have gone to the bank many times" or "The cats have already eaten."

1. (   ) Mr. Lee _____   6. (   ) you _____

2. (   ) she _____   7. (   ) she _____

3. (   ) the teacher _____   8. (   ) Sue and Jo _____

4. (   ) you _____   9. (   ) you _____

5. (   ) April _____   10. (   ) we _____

CHALLENGE
1. I don't have a car.
2. I haven't had a car since 1976.
3. *Bill:* "Are you hungry?"
   Sam: "Yes, I am. I haven't eaten anything all day."
4. I haven't a pencil.

All of these sentences have a negative verb. Which one of these sentences is unusual in North American English? Why is it unusual? What is the rule?

Usage No. 1: Recent Past Action That Is Important to Now

Example   *Key Words*

Amber: It's hot in here. Why don't you turn on the air conditioner?

James: Actually, I**'ve** just **turned*** it on. We have to wait a few   just
minutes to feel it. Can I help you with the reports?

Amber: Thanks, but I**'ve** already **finished*** them. Here they are.   already

Note: We can use present perfect to talk about a past action that happened a short time ago and that is still important to the current situation. In this example, Amber is complaining about the temperature in the room right now. James explains to Amber that he has turned on the air conditioner. When James uses **has turned on**, this means that the action is finished but that it is still important to the current situation. In other words, there is a connection between his action and the current situation in the room. This kind of sentence often uses the word **just** to show that the action just happened.

*Simple past tense can be used here without changing the meaning.

Exercise 8.   Practice using *just*, present perfect, and contractions in these dialogues, using the following words.

          finish   realize   come   cook   take   run

1. *Sam:*   I _____ some spaghetti. Would you like some?

    Dean: No, thanks. I _____ eating lunch.

    Sam: OK, but if you change your mind, be sure to let me know.

2. *Pete:*   Hey, the next time that you go to the post office, would you pick up some

            stamps for me?

    Gwen: Why, of course, but it's too bad you didn't ask me sooner. I

            _____ back from the post office.

3. *Keith:*   Hey, Jim. Can you give me a ride to the store now?

    Jim: I'm sorry, but my car _____ out of gas. Why don't you

               ask Sandy for a ride? I think she's about to go★ home.

4. *Woman:*   Excuse me, sir. Has flight 663 left yet?

    Man: Yes, it _____ off. Why do you ask?

    Woman: Well, I _____ that I left my carry-on bag on the plane.

    Man: No problem. Here it is. Someone found it and turned it in to us.

★*be + about to* + VERB = The action is going to happen very soon.
It's about to rain. (The sky is very dark.)
Careful! You're about to drop those books. (The person isn't holding the books tightly.)

Usage No. 2: Past Experience, Indefinite Past Time

Example   *Key Words*

Katie: Susan has just gotten back from China. She told me she
           had a great time.
Sean: That's wonderful news. She must be tired. That was
           really a long trip.
Katie: I wonder how many hours it is from here to China. **Have**
           you ever **gone** there?   ever
Sean: No, I**'ve** never **gone** there, but my uncle **has traveled**   never
           there many times. In fact, he <u>went</u> there last month. He has many times
           to go there on business.   (others: before,
                                                                               already)

Note: We can use present perfect to talk about a past experience. In this situation, one
person wants to know if a second person has ever done a particular action. In this example, Katie is telling Sean that Susan has just returned from China. Katie wants to know
if Sean has ever traveled to China. She uses the common question, "Have you ever . . . ?"
Notice that <u>went</u> is in simple past tense because it refers to a specific past event. In other
words, it refers to definite past time, not indefinite past time. You will practice this move
from present perfect to past tense in exercises 10 and 14.

Exercise 9. Practice using present perfect and contractions in these dialogues. Add *ever* in questions. Add *never* in the answers if it is appropriate. Use the following words.

have   think   hear   study   have   eat   be   travel

1. *Emily:* _____ tempura?

   Laura: No, I haven't. What is it?

   Emily: It's a Japanese dish. It's fried vegetables or fried fish.

   Laura: Really? I _____ of it.

   Emily: You ought to try it. It's great.

2. *Vic:* _____ a foreign language?

   Carl: Yes, I studied French when I was in college.

   Vic: _____ a chance to use it? I mean,

   _____ to France?

   Carl: Unfortunately, no. I _____ abroad.

3. *Ben:* I'm sorry I'm late, but I had car trouble again this morning.

   Jean: Why do you keep that old car? _____ about getting a

   new car?

   Ben: Sure, I've thought about it, but I _____ enough money

   to buy one.

Speaking Activity

Exercise 10. Speaking Activity

Step 1. Work with a partner.

You are at a meeting or party, and there are sixteen people in the room. You will be one of these sixteen people. You have done four special things that no one else in the room has done. Choose a person that you will be, but do NOT let your partner know your choice.

Step 2. Take turns asking *yes-no* questions to try to guess your partner's four special things.

If the answer to a question is YES, the answerer has to make up an extra sentence to add to the conversation. This extra information should probably be in the past tense. In English conversation, it is common to move from present perfect (general information) to past tense (specific information).

If the answer is YES, then the questioner can continue asking. If the answer is NO, the turn passes to the other student. Remember to use "Have you ever. . . ?" in your conversations. Practice English grammar!

Step 3.   The first partner to finish is the winner! (You can't use people's names until the end!)

example: A: Have you ever been to France?★

B: No, I have never gone to France. (So it's B's turn to ask a question.)

B: Have you ever been on an elephant?

A: Yes, I've been on an elephant. I went to Thailand in 1985, and I rode an elephant there. (So B continues asking.)

B: Have you ever gone to Egypt?

A: No, I haven't gone to Egypt. (So it's A's turn again to ask a question.)

★ In the perfect tenses, *be* can sometimes be used instead of *go.* Thus, "I've been to France" is a common way of saying "I've gone to France." However, we can only use this structure in the perfect tenses. We cannot use it in simple past tense. We cannot say, "I was to France." In this case, we must say, "I went to France."

Shirley	*Charlotte*	*Mary*	*Troy*
went to France flew on a 747 drove a BMW was on a horse	went to France flew on a 747 drove a Toyota truck was on a horse	went to France flew on the Concorde drove a BMW was on a horse	went to France flew on the Concorde drove a Toyota truck was on a horse
Cindy	*James*	*Simon*	*Kevin*
went to France flew on a 747 drove a BMW was on an elephant	went to France flew on a 747 drove a Toyota truck was on an elephant	went to France flew on the Concorde drove a BMW was on an elephant	went to France flew on the Concorde drove a Toyota truck was on an elephant
Chris	*Mark*	*Silvia*	*Terri*
went to Egypt flew on a 747 drove a BMW was on a horse	went to Egypt flew on a 747 drove a Toyota truck was on a horse	went to Egypt flew on the Concorde drove a BMW was on a horse	went to Egypt flew on the Concorde drove a Toyota truck was on a horse
Melissa	*Anne*	*Jan*	*Lucas*
went to Egypt flew on a 747 drove a BMW was on an elephant	went to Egypt flew on a 747 drove a Toyota truck was on an elephant	went to Egypt flew on the Concorde drove a BMW was on an elephant	went to Egypt flew on the Concorde drove a Toyota truck was on an elephant

Usage No. 3: Past Action or Situation that Continues Now

Example   *Key Words*

José: How long **have** you **worked** at Carpet World?   how long

Sara: I**'ve been** there for eighteen years. In fact, I**'ve worked**   for★
          there longer than any of my supervisors!

José: What do you do there?

Sara: I used to work on the assembly line, but since 1995, I**'ve**   since★
          been with the sales force in the front office.

José: Have you ever met the president of the corporation?

Sara: Actually, no, I**'ve** never **met** him. He never comes to the office.   never (= a past
                                                                             action that
                                                                             continues)

Note: We can use present perfect to talk about a past action or situation that continues
now. (It can be affirmative or negative; the important thing is that it still continues.) In this
example, Sara tells José that she has been at this same company for eighteen years. This
means that the action began eighteen years ago and still continues today.

★Use **since** + the name of the time and **for** + the duration of the time.
I've lived here since 1995. I've lived here for six years.

Exercise 11.   Write *since* or *for* on the line. Follow the examples.

1. __since__ yesterday   5. _____ two months   9. _____ one minute

2. __for__ six weeks   6. _____ noon   10. _____ a decade

3. _____ six o'clock   7. _____ a few days   11. _____ 1993

4. _____ March   8. _____ my birthday   12. _____ late last night

---

Exercise 12.   Read the two sentences and then write a new sentence using *since*
                     or *for*. Follow the examples.

          example: I live on Madison Avenue. I moved there five months ago.

                      ___I have lived on Madison Avenue for five months.___

          I live on Madison Avenue. I moved there in 1970.

                      ___I have lived on Madison Avenue since 1970.___

1. Apples are on sale. The sale started on Monday.

   _____

2. Yolanda owns a BMW. She bought it in 1997.

   _____

3. We know the mayor. We met her ten years ago.

   _____

4. I began to work at this office two years ago. I still work here.

   _____

5. Henry has a huge house. He purchased it when he moved here.

   _____

6. Keith plays tennis. He learned how to play in 1982.

   _____

7. Mrs. deMontluzin teaches French. Her first year was 1991.

   _____

8. Dr. Lorraine is a university professor. She began that job in the fall of 1995.

   _____

CHALLENGE   A student wrote, "I've begun to work here since 1994."

The grammar in this sentence is wrong. Write three variations using these time expressions: *in 1994, since 1994, for* (this year minus 1994) *years.*

Usage No. 4: With *Yet*

Example		*Key Words*
Mike:	We don't have much time. Are you almost through?★	
Kent:	Give me just a few more minutes, Mike.	
Mike:	What about the travel report and the salary sheets?	
	Have you **finished** them yet?	yet (in a question)
Kent:	I've already finished the salary sheets, but I **haven't finished** the travel report yet. I only need a few more minutes, OK?	yet (in a negative)

★be through = be finished

Note: We might use present perfect with **yet** in a question to show that we expect the action to be finished soon. We use present perfect with **yet** in a negative statement to show that the action is a little late or that it should be finished soon.

Have you bought your ticket yet?
I haven't done the homework yet. (= I admit I'm late; OR I'll do it soon.)
It hasn't rained yet. (= The sky is black; OR The weather report has predicted rain for today.)

Exercise 13. Read the situation and then write a negative sentence with *yet.* Follow the example.

Situation 1. Ben always eats dinner at 7:00 P.M. It's 6:45 P.M. now.

_____Ben hasn't eaten dinner yet._____

Situation 2. The weather report predicted rain for today. The sky is dark, but the ground is dry.

_____

Situation 3. The monitor says the plane will arrive in ten minutes. The plane is still in the air.

_____

Situation 4. We are all very hungry. The stew is on the stove. It needs to cook some more.

_____

Situation 5. I wanted to speak with Dr. Adams yesterday, but I didn't have time. I need to speak to him.

_____

Situation 6. The big game is tomorrow. I forgot to buy my ticket this morning. I need a ticket!

_____

Usage No. 5: With a Superlative

Example   *Key Words*

Saleh: How was the movie that you went to see last night?
Marcos: Don't waste your money! That was the worst movie that   the worst
           I **have** ever **seen** in my life.
Saleh: Wow, I'm surprised. You know it's the most expensive   the most
           movie that anyone in Hollywood **has** ever **made**.   expensive

Note: We usually use present perfect with a superlative. When we say that a movie is the best, we mean that it is the best that we have seen up to that point in time.

Speaking Activity
(( ))

Exercise 14. Speaking Activity

Write five questions practicing superlative + *ever* + present perfect. Use the words given below. Write your five questions. Write your own answers on the first answer line (S1). Then interview a classmate. Take turns asking each other questions.* Write down your partner's answers on the second answer line (S2). Follow the example.

The Princess Bride

example: (really bad) movie / see

[?]   ___Have you ever seen a really bad movie?___

S1:   ___Yes, I have. It was <u>Jaws</u>. I hated it.___

S2:   _____

1. (incredibly long) trip / take

   [?] _____

   S1: _____

   S2: _____

2. (really good) food / eat

   [?] _____

   S1: _____

   S2: _____

*If you want, continue the conversation if you get a YES answer. Ask more questions about that situation or topic. Note that almost all of the subsequent questions will be in the past tense. Therefore, one of the things that present perfect does is to connect a past event to the present first by present perfect and second by past tense. Note the shift from present perfect to past tense.

3. (amazingly beautiful) place / visit

[?] _____

S1: _____

S2: _____

4. (extremely interesting) book / read

[?] _____

S1: _____

S2: _____

5. (incredibly easy) job / have

[?] _____

S1: _____

S2: _____

Usage No. 6: *The First . . . , The Third . . .*

Example		*Key Words*
Mother:	Is that the third paper that you **have had** to write for that class this semester?	that is the third . . .
Bernadette:	Yes, but it's the first paper that the teacher **has asked** us to complete on the computer.	it is the first . . .
Mother:	So what are you worried about now?	
Bernadette:	I'm not good at using the computer.	
Mother:	You have to practice! This seems like the hundredth time that **I've told** you that you need to practice!	the hundredth time

Note: When we say, "It's the first paper that he's asked us to complete on the computer," we are connecting all the past papers to the present paper, so we use present perfect because present perfect connects a past event and the present.

1. It's the first job that **I've** really **liked**.
2. The first job that I **liked** was my job at IBM.

Why does the first sentence use present perfect but the second one uses past tense?

Exercise 15.   Underline the correct verb form.

1. *Andy:*   Here's today's newspaper.

    Sue: Andy, this is not today's paper. This is the second time

              that you (gave, have given) me yesterday's paper.

2. *Koji:*   Can you remember the first time that you (met, have

              met) Tim?

    Beth: Yes, I can. It (was, has been) 1993. We (were, have been)

              both in high school.

3. *Gina:*   I don't know if I'll ever be able to remember all these people's names! It's the

              third day that I (saw, have seen) Frank and Tony, but I still have trouble

              remembering their names.

    Wes: Don't worry about it. I'm not very good with names either.

4. *Coach:* Lim, is there a problem? That is the fourth time that you (dropped, have

              dropped) a ball in this game. Are you trying to set a new record?

    Lim: Sorry, coach. My mind is somewhere else today.

Usage No. 7: Repetition of an Action before Now
(exact time is not important)

Example	*Key Words*
Weiping: Can you believe it? There's another test next Monday!	
Paolo: Yeah, it's crazy. We**'ve had** six tests so far this month.	six . . . so far
Weiping: You know, in my biology class, the teacher **has given** only one test this semester.	one . . . this semester
Paolo: Well, that's not good either. If you did badly on that one test, then your grade for the course is in trouble.	
Weiping: Maybe so, but I**'ve had** a lot of classes like that here.	a lot

Note: It is common to use present perfect to talk about the number of times that you have
done something. In these sentences, the idea is that there is still a possibility that the action
or event may happen again. We do not use this if the time period is finished. The three

present perfect examples above refer to this month, this semester, and Weiping's time as a student at this school. All three of these time periods are still continuing. We could not use present perfect if the time periods were last month, last semester, or when Weiping was a student in high school.

Comparing Simple Past Tense and Present Perfect Tense

CAREFUL! Do not make these common mistakes.

1. Do not use present perfect with any specific past tense time words.
   wrong: I have gone to Mexico several times when I was in college.
   correct: I went to Mexico several times when I was in college.

   wrong: In 1998, *Titantic* has become the most popular movie ever.
   correct: In 1998, *Titantic* became the most popular movie ever.

2. Do not use simple past tense with time expressions that mean "until now."
   wrong: We wrote six papers in this class so far. When will the work end?
   correct: We have written six papers in this class so far. When will the work end?

3. Do not use simple past tense with actions that are still continuing.
   wrong: I lived in this same apartment since 1996.
   correct: I have lived in this same apartment since 1996.

CHALLENGE

1. I have written two letters this week.
2. I wrote two letters this week.
3. I have written two letters last week.
4. I wrote two letters last week.

One of these sentences is not correct. Identify the incorrect sentence and tell why it is wrong. Can you explain the difference between the other sentences?

Exercise 16. Put a check mark (√) by the expressions to show if they are only for past tense, only for present perfect tense, or possible with both. Follow the examples.

	Past Only	Present Perfect Only	Both OK	
1.	✔	____	____	in 1995
2.	____	✔	____	so far
3.	____	____	✔	today
4.	____	____	____	until now
5.	____	____	____	just
6.	____	____	____	for the last two years
7.	____	____	____	for two years

	Past Only	Present Perfect Only	Both OK	
8.	____	____	____	last month
9.	____	____	____	ever
10.	____	____	____	since Monday
11.	____	____	____	a week ago
12.	____	____	____	never
13.	____	____	____	at noon
14.	____	____	____	before the class

Exercise 17. Read the statement and then write the verb in parentheses in the correct tense. Use simple past or present perfect. Follow the examples.

(go)   1. I _____have gone_____ to Mexico many times, and

I hope to go again some day.

2. I _____went_____ to Mexico in 1996 and 1997.

(eat)   3. _____ you ever _____ octopus?

4. When you lived in Japan, _____ you ever _____

octopus?

(see)   5. Did you like that movie the first time that you _____ it?

6. This is the first time that I _____ a movie with that

actor.

(have) 7. The people who live here _____ a lot of parties this year.

8. In fact, the people who live here _____ a party last night.

(fly)   9. The last time that you went to New York, _____ you _____ on

United Airlines?

10. How many times _____ you _____ on United Airlines?

Exercise 18.   Write the verb in parentheses in past tense or present perfect tense according to the situation. Some of the blanks will not have any word. Follow the example.

1. *Greg:* (call) I ____called____ your house last night, but there was no answer. (be)

      Where __were__ you __—__?

  Hank: (be) I ____was____ at the library. (be) In fact, I __have been__ there

      every day this week because I have to finish this research paper.

2. *Joe:* (work) _____ you _____ at Ford for a long time?

  Sue: Oh, didn't you hear the news? (retire) I _____ last month.

  Joe: (work) Well, how long _____ you _____ there?

  Sue: (work) I _____ there for eighteen years. (be) In fact, I

      _____ there longer than any of my supervisors!

3. *Anna:* (go) Mark, _____ you ever _____ to Africa?

  Mark: Yes, I have. (travel) I _____ there several times.

  Anna: (go) When was the last time that you _____ there?

  Mark: (go, be) The last time I _____ there _____ in 1997.

  Anna: (stay) How long _____ you _____ there?

  Mark: For two weeks.

4. *Cal:* Why did you come to Florida?

  Alan: I came here to get a better job.

  Cal: (be) How long _____ you _____ here?

  Alan: Almost ten years.

  Cal: (be) Before you came to Florida, where _____ you _____?

  Alan: (be) I _____ in Japan. (have) I _____ a job there.

  Cal: (work) Really? How long _____ you _____ there?

  Alan: Six years.

Exercise 19.   Multiple Choice. Circle the letter of the correct answers.

1. "So how long _____ there? I can't believe you're still there!"

   "Well, I started there in 1960. You do the math."

   (A) do you work   (C) have you worked

   (B) did you work   (D) are you working

2. "Have you ever _____ anything important?"

   "No, never."

   (A) won   (C) stole

   (B) build   (D) make

3. "How many movies do you think you _____ in your life?"

   (A) ever see   (C) have ever seen

   (B) ever saw   (D) are ever seen

4. I don't have a car now. In fact, I _____ a car since 1996.

   (A) haven't had   (C) don't have

   (B) didn't have   (D) didn't had

5. "My stomach hurts."

   "I _____ some medicine yesterday. Would you like some?"

   (A) have bought   (C) was buying

   (B) was buying   (D) bought

6. We've discussed our ideas for the meeting _____ the past month, so it's time to

   make a decision.

   (A) for   (C) since

   (B) by   (D) with

7. "Do you know Rob Douglas?"

   "Why of course I do. I _____ him a long time."

   (A) have met   (C) met

   (B) have known   (D) known

8. "Hi, I'm here to pick up the checks for my department staff."

   "I'm sorry, but you're a little bit early. They're not ready _____."

   (A) yet   (C) already

   (B) some   (D) all

Exercise 20.   Review Test

Part 1.   Fill in the blanks with the correct tense of the verb in parentheses.

1. *Dot:*   Hey, what are you doing?

    Adele: I'm cooking dinner. Why? Don't you want to eat?

    Dot: (make) Yes, but I _____ already _____ plans to eat out with Mike.

2. (take)   Every year my wife and I _____ a trip to Colorado in the summer. However, this year is different. (decide) This is the first year that we _____ not to go to Colorado. Instead, we are considering going to California or to Quebec. (be) My wife _____ never _____ to California, (go) but I _____ there in 1995. (travel) Neither of us _____ outside the U.S., so a trip to Quebec would be special for both of us.

3. *Joe:*   What happened? (bleed) Your finger _____!

    Mike: Oh, it's nothing. (cut) I _____ some potatoes (cut) when I accidentally _____ myself. Don't worry about it. It may look bad, but it's just a little cut.

    Joe: (do) _____ you ever _____ this before?

    Mike: Well . . . I'm not very good at cutting and cooking. (happen) Yes, it _____ before.

Part 2.   Read each sentence carefully. Look at the underlined part. If the underlined part is correct, circle the word *correct*. If it is wrong, circle the wrong part and write the correct form above.

correct   wrong   1. I <u>have met</u> Dr. Smith for at least ten years.

correct   wrong   2. The last time I <u>have gone</u> to France was in 1997.

correct   wrong   3. <u>Have you ever taken</u> a train for a very long trip?

correct   wrong   4. I can't leave with you right now. I haven't finished this work <u>still</u>.

correct   wrong   5. Karen used to work in this office, but since 1994, she <u>worked</u> in the
accounting office.

correct   wrong   6. I <u>finished</u> cooking dinner about an hour ago. The food is on the
stove. Please help yourself.

correct   wrong   7. George is not new to this city. In fact, he <u>has</u> over ten years here.

correct   wrong   8. We<u>'ve seen that movie already</u>, but we didn't really like it.

Quiz Practices

Quiz 1.   Write the missing past and past participle forms.

Present	Past	Past Participle	Present	Past	Past Participle
1. be	_____	_____	11. lose	_____	_____
2. make	_____	_____	12. see	_____	_____
3. forget	_____	_____	13. freeze	_____	_____
4. show	_____	_____	14. sing	_____	_____
5. sit	_____	_____	15. sleep	_____	_____
6. hit	_____	_____	16. leave	_____	_____
7. steal	_____	_____	17. swim	_____	_____
8. take	_____	_____	18. teach	_____	_____
9. tell	_____	_____	19. break	_____	_____
10. think	_____	_____	20. run	_____	_____

Quiz 2.   Write the missing past and past participle forms.

Present	Past	Past Participle	Present	Past	Past Participle
1. say	_____	_____	6. speak	_____	_____
2. wear	_____	_____	7. buy	_____	_____
3. write	_____	_____	8. catch	_____	_____
4. begin	_____	_____	9. drink	_____	_____
5. ride	_____	_____	10. eat	_____	_____

Present	Past	Past Participle	Present	Past	Past Participle
11. choose			16. spend		
12. win			17. put		
13. become			18. meet		
14. bring			19. drive		
15. come			20. fall		

Quiz 3. Write the missing past and past participle forms.

Present	Past	Past Participle	Present	Past	Past Participle
1. feel			11. do		
2. find			12. lend		
3. sell			13. send		
4. hold			14. read		
5. keep			15. know		
6. cost			16. cut		
7. let			17. fly		
8. get			18. give		
9. go			19. have		
10. build			20. understand		

Extra Writing Practice

Situation: You are in a foreign country. You have been there two or three months. A good friend of yours has just found out that you are in this country. She didn't know that you were not in your native country now. Your friend wrote you the following letter. Write a reply to your friend's letter.

Be sure to practice the present perfect tense. Try to use present perfect at least five times and simple past tense at least five times. For example, you might write, "How <u>have you been</u>?" or "I didn't know you weren't here. How long <u>have you been</u> there?" Always underline the grammar point that you have used so the teacher can see what you are trying to practice.

Dear (your name),

Hi, how are you doing? What are you doing in [the country that you want]? I was talking to our good friend Susan last night, and she mentioned very casually that you were in [the country]. I couldn't believe it! How come★ I didn't know?

So how long have you been there? Do you like it? What are you doing there? Why did you go there? Why didn't I know that you were going there? How long are you going to stay?

I never thought that you were the kind of person who would want to live in a foreign country. What is the country like? What are the people like? What is the strangest thing that you have seen there?

I'm full of questions, and I hope you are full of answers! Write me back as soon as you can. I want to know how you've been.

Your friend,
Patricia

★ *Note to Advanced Students: how come* means *why;* however, the grammar for *how come* is unique. We do not use inverted word order or auxiliary verbs.

Why are you late?	=	How come you are late?
Why did you call?	=	How come you called?

Unit 5

Adverbs of Manner and Related Terms

1. form: ADJECTIVE + -*ly*
2. *by* + — vs. *with* + —
3. *by* + VERB + -*ing*

Adverbs of Manner

Adjective	*Adverb*
He is a **quick** reader.	He can read **quickly**.
They are **careful** workers.	They work **carefully**.
We are **fluent** speakers of English.	We speak English **fluently**.
I want to use the **correct** words when I speak.	I want to speak **correctly**.
Her typing ability is **good**.	She types **well**.

Remember: 1. Adjectives talk about nouns or pronouns.
Adverbs talk about the action of the verb.

> *example:* He is a **quiet** <u>person</u>.
> adjective noun
> (**quiet** talks about **person**)
> He always <u>works</u> very **quietly**.
> verb adverb
> (**quietly** talks about how he works)

2. Adverbs of manner usually end in the letters **-ly.**★
exceptions: **fast, hard, well, loud**

3. Adjectives can come before a noun or after the verb **be**.
Adverbs of manner usually come after an action verb.
adjective: He is a quiet worker. He is quiet.
adverb: He works quietly.

Adjective	*Adverb of Manner*
clear	clearly
correct	correctly
easy	easily
fluent	fluently
nervous	nervously
quick	quickly
slow	slowly
rapid	rapidly
(exceptions)	
fast	fast
good	well
hard	hard
loud	loud(ly)

★ There are some words that end in **-ly,** but they are not adverbs of manner. These words are adjectives. Examples are **friendly, likely, lovely.**

examples: She is a very <u>friendly</u> person. (**friendly** is an adjective)
The radio said that tomorrow rain is <u>likely</u>. (**likely** is an adjective)
Emily's new baby is a <u>lovely</u> child. (**lovely** is an adjective)

The word **hardly** ends in **-ly,** but it is not an adverb of manner. It is an adverb of frequency and means "rarely, almost never." It does not mean "very much" or "very strongly."
wrong: He is a good student. He studies <u>hardly</u>.
correct: He is a good student. He studies <u>hard</u>. (**hard** is an adverb of manner)
correct: He is a bad student. He <u>hardly</u> studies. (**hardly** is an adverb of frequency)

CAREFUL! Do not make these common mistakes.

1. Do not use adjective forms when you should use an adverb form.
   wrong: He plays tennis really good.
   correct: He plays tennis really well.

2. Do not confuse *hard* and *hardly*.
   wrong: She studied really hardly for the final exam in history.
   correct: She studied really hard for the final exam in history.

Exercise 1.   Write the adverb form for these adjectives. Follow the examples.

examples: correct ____*correctly*____   real ____*really*____

1. quick   _____   11. hard   _____
2. sudden   _____   12. rapid   _____
3. sincere   _____   13. poor   _____
4. silent   _____   14. furious   _____
5. happy   _____   15. sad   _____
6. fast   _____   16. prompt   _____
7. punctual   _____   17. careful   _____
8. good   _____   18. bad   _____
9. enormous   _____   19. huge   _____
10. wise   _____   20. stupid   _____

Exercise 2.   One sentence is an example of an adjective. The other sentence is an example of an adverb form of the same adjective. Fill in the missing words. Follow the examples.

Adjective	*Adverb*
1. He is a quiet worker.	_*He works quietly.*_
2. _*She is a slow eater.*_	She eats slowly.
3. Mark is a very fast swimmer.	_____
4. They are good singers.	_____
5. _____	They work really carefully.

6. Joy is a quick runner.   _____

7. _____   Tim speaks Thai fluently.

8. _____   Keith doesn't sing very well.

Exercise 3.   Underline the correct adjective or adverb form. Follow the example.

> *example:*   The little boy (quick, <u>quickly</u>) ran to the door to see who was
>   there.

1. Our piano teacher always praises (good, well) performances.

2. The (rapid, rapidly) decline in the value of the yen is making many people (nervous, nervously).

3. The sky was very (dark, darkly), and then it (sudden, suddenly) started to rain (hard, hardly).

4. The coach made a (wise, wisely) decision when he took Karen out of the game because she was playing rather (poor, poorly) yesterday.

5. He said the answer (nervous, nervously), so we didn't know if he knew the (correct, correctly) answer or not.

6. She has such a (good, well) voice. It's certainly (easy, easily) to listen to someone who can sing so (beautiful, beautifully).

7. Ms. Tran's (clear, clearly) explanations helped me to get (high, highly) scores on the university entrance exam.

8. I worked as (rapid, rapidly) as I could, but I tried to be (careful, carefully), too.

Exercise 4.   Editing. Circle the six adjective or adverb mistakes in this paragraph. (The first one has already been done for you.)

   Two very (dangerously) prisoners escaped from the city jail last night. Police have reported that Arthur Henson and Miles Smith hit a prison guard on the head with a largely rock and then ran into the wooded area behind the jail. When the guard fell down, he managed to touch an alarm button, so between eight and twelve officers arrived on the scene instantly. This specially group immediately began to search the huge area behind the jail. Two of the officers saw one of the prisoners crouching quiet behind a tree. When the officers shouted, "Stop or we'll shoot," the prisoner surrendered rather easy. Unless the other prisoner is a very cleverly person, police think that they'll be able to catch him as well.

By and *With*

We use **by** + NOUN and **with** + NOUN to tell HOW something was done. Study these examples to have a better understanding of this grammar.

by

1. *A:* How did you go there?
   B: I went by plane.
2. *A:* How did you get the information?
   B: He sent it to me by fax.

By tells the means or method of doing something. Note that most of the words that we use with **by** are forms of communication or transportation.

The noun that is used with **by** does not have an article **(a, an, the)** with it; this is contrary to the usual rules for count nouns.

with

3. *A:* How did you get in the house?
   B: I got in with an old key.
4. *A:* Do people in your country use forks?
   B: We usually eat with our hands.

With is used with an instrument or . means. **With** can be followed by an article and other words.

CAREFUL! Watch out for these common mistakes.

1. Do not use the wrong preposition.
   wrong: He went there with his car.
   correct: He went there by car.

2. Do not use an article or determiner or possessive word with **by**.
   wrong: Sarah paid by her credit card.
   correct: Sarah paid by credit card.

Exercise 5. Write *by* or *with* on the line. Follow the examples.

1. __by__ telegraph 6. _____ airmail 11. _____ train

2. __with__ a smile 7. _____ a nod 12. _____ hand

3. _____ a silver key 8. _____ a can opener 13. _____ his right hand

4. _____ e-mail 9. _____ fax 14. _____ taxi

5. _____ a new pen 10. _____ a gesture 15. _____ land

Exercise 6. Write *by* or *with* on the lines. Follow the example.

1. *Ann:* Did you take these pictures __with__ your new camera?

   Paul: Yes, I did. That's a great camera.

   Ann: But it's really expensive. How did you manage to

   pay for it?★

   Paul: I paid for it _____ a credit card, so I still have

   a few weeks until I have to pay for it.

2. *Jack:* This is my first time to go to Europe.

   Hank: And you're going _____ ship. You're so lucky.

   Jack: Lucky? I wish we were going _____ plane.

   Traveling _____ ship does not seem so nice.

3. *Fran:* Staying in touch _____ telephone is certainly easier nowadays.

   Greg: I couldn't agree with you more, but my sister and I communicate

   _____ e-mail almost every day.

4. *Luke:* Can I pay for this _____ check?

   Clerk: You can use a check if you want. You can also pay _____ credit card.

5. *Zina:* Did Julia drive there _____ friends?

   Wes: No, they went there _____ bus.

★Asking about money matters is very personal. We can assume that Ann and Paul are close friends or relatives
if they are discussing this matter so openly.

by + VERB + -ing

We use **by + VERB + -ing** to tell HOW something was done. Study these examples to have a better understanding of this grammar point.

A: How did you make such a high score on the TOEFL?

B: By reading magazines and newspapers and by speaking English as often as possible.

A: What is your company's plan for future growth?

B: By opening eight new stores every year, we hope to be the number one store in this state by the year 2010.

CAREFUL! Watch out for these common mistakes.

1. Do not forget to use **by** in this grammar construction.
   beginner: He studied very hard every day. He passed the test.
   advanced: He passed the test by studying very hard every day.

2. Do not use the wrong verb form.
   wrong: Julia learned English by listen to the radio every night.
   correct: Julia learned English by listening to the radio every night.

3. Do not use **don't**, **doesn't**, or **didn't** with this grammar construction.
   wrong: You made the teacher angry by don't coming to class on time.
   correct: You made the teacher angry by not coming to class on time.

4. Do not confuse **to + VERB** with **VERB + -ing.** We use **to + VERB** (or **in order to + VERB**) to tell why; we use **VERB + -ing** to tell how.
   How did you learn to speak Italian?
   wrong: To listen to cassettes every evening.
   correct: By listening to cassettes every evening.

   Why did you learn Italian?
   wrong: By getting a job with an Italian company.
   correct: To get a job with an Italian company.
   correct: In order to get a job with an Italian company.

Exercise 7.   Write the correct form of one of the verbs on the line. Follow the example.

step   say   search   take   work   count   write   fry

1. Billy learned the new vocabulary by ____saying____ each word aloud five times.

2. Mrs. Prince cooked the chicken by _____ it in olive oil.

3. Some people fall asleep by _____ sheep.

4. Our teacher always begins every class by _____ the date on the blackboard.

5. He hurt his foot seriously by _____ on a piece of glass.

6. We saved some money by _____ the later flight.

7. Frank found a good job by _____ in the newspaper.

8. I got enough money to buy a used car by _____ two jobs for a year.

Exercise 8.   Answer the question. Try to use *by* + VERB + *-ing* in your answer.

1. How can students learn English quickly?

_____

2. How can people lose weight?

_____

3. How can drivers avoid accidents?

_____

4. How can someone learn to cook well?

_____

5. How can you find a place when you're lost?

_____

6. How can students improve their pronunciation quickly?

_____

Exercise 9.   Underline the correct verb form. Follow the example.

1. She learned to play the piano so well (<u>by practicing</u>, to practice) every day.

2. We cut up the onions (by making, to make) stew.

3. They lost their wallets (by not being, not to be) careful.

4. I learned the words (by repeating, to repeat) them out loud.

5. I learned the words (by passing, to pass) the exam.

6. We stopped the car a few minutes (by making, to make) a phone call.

7. The teacher told the students to read the article (by finding, to find) out the surprise ending.

8. She opened the window (by letting, to let) some fresh air in.

Speaking Activity

Exercise 10.   Speaking Activity: Role Play

1. Work with a partner. Choose one of the situations below.

Situation A. One of you is an expert language teacher. The other one is a newspaper reporter. In this interview, the reporter is trying to find out some of the best ways for students to learn English as quickly as possible. Be sure to ask how to learn vocabulary or how to improve reading skills, etc.

Situation B. One of you is an expert cook. The other one is a reporter for a cooking magazine. In this interview, the reporter wants to find out the best ways to cook three kinds of food (for example, chicken, pasta, and fish). The reporter needs to write about recipes that are healthy, so be sure to ask how to cook these dishes without much oil or without salt, etc.

2. Write an interview that has at least three questions and answers. Be sure to include examples of the grammar from this unit: VERB + -*ing*, adverbs of manner (-*ly*), and *by/with* + NOUN.

3. When you finish, take turns presenting your interviews to the class. Everyone should pay special attention to the *by* + -*ing* constructions and to the use of adverbs of manner.

_____

_____

_____

_____

_____

_____

_____

_____

_____

_____

Exercise 11.   Multiple Choice. Circle the letter of the correct answer.

1. There was a _____ noise, and then we heard someone open the door.

   (A) by sudden   (C) suddenly

   (B) with sudden   (D) sudden

2. "I got another speeding ticket yesterday."

   "That's awful. If you don't drive more _____, you're going to have an accident."

   (A) careful   (C) carefully

   (B) care   (D) with care

3. "So how did he send you the money so quickly?"

   "He sent it _____ wire."

   (A) by   (C) for

   (B) at   (D) with

4. "Julia's pronunciation in English is excellent, isn't it?"

   "Yes, it is. She improved it by _____ to cassettes day after day."

   (A) listen   (C) to listen

   (B) listening   (D) listened

5. "_____ did you lose so much weight?"

   "By exercising every morning before I went to work."

   (A) Why   (C) What

   (B) Which   (D) How

6. The speed skater finished the race _____ a smile. She knew that she might win.

   (A) by   (C) for

   (B) at   (D) with

7. "Wow, Luke is a very good singer."

   "That's true, but his cousin Anne can sing _____, too."

   (A) good   (C) well

   (B) hardly   (D) likely

8. "How did you get ideas for decorating your house?"

   "_____ at lots of magazines."

   (A) To looking   (C) To look

   (B) By looking   (D) By look

Exercise 12.   Review Test

Part 1.   Read these sentences. Fill in the blanks with *by* or *with*.

1. *Sam:*   How did you get such a good deal on this car?

    Bob: _____ doing a little research on the computer.

    Sam: What do you mean?

    Bob: I found out the real price of the car _____

    searching the web. Then I contacted a car company and they sent me some

    information _____ e-mail.

    Sam: So you were able to find out everything _____ your old computer?

    Bob: It may be old, but it works just fine.

2. *Cindy:* I need to get this package to New York for a meeting tomorrow.

    Wes: Then you'll have to send it _____ overnight delivery.

    Cindy: But isn't that expensive? I don't have any cash right now.

    Wes: Well, it isn't cheap, but the package will be there tomorrow, and you

    can pay _____ credit card.

Part 2.   Circle the correct word.

1. If you call Peter (quick, quickly), there's a chance he still might be home.
2. In order to play golf (good, well), you have to practice every day.
3. He was running so (hard, hardly) that he couldn't even talk.
4. There are always lots of birds on the beach when we have (clear, clearly)
   weather.

Part 3.   Read each sentence carefully. Look at the underlined part. If the
underlined part is correct, circle the word *correct*. If it is wrong, circle the
wrong part and write the correct form above.

correct   wrong   1. He learned to speak Spanish <u>by watching</u> Spanish movies.

correct   wrong   2. I wrote my boss a letter <u>to complain</u> about my salary.

correct   wrong   3. You can pay <u>by credit card or by check</u>.

correct   wrong   4. If the company receives your payment <u>lately</u>, you have to pay an

    extra ten percent.

correct   wrong   5. <u>By no arriving</u> to the interview on time, Joe lost a chance of getting a great job.

correct   wrong   6. The best way to cook broccoli is by <u>fry</u> it in sesame seed oil.

correct   wrong   7. <u>By driving</u> to Boston, we were able to see many small towns.

correct   wrong   8. <u>To drive</u> to Boston, we had to drive through many small towns.

Extra Writing Practice

Situation: A friend has written a letter to you in which she asks you how to make (the name of a kind of food). Your grandmother taught your mother and your mother taught you how to make this dish. Write a small note to your friend telling how to make this dish.

Be sure to practice several of the grammar items from this unit. Be sure to include at least three adverbs of manner and three descriptive adjectives.★ Try to use *with* + NOUN and *by* + NOUN and *by* + GERUND in your reply. For example, you might write, "You should make this meat sauce <u>with</u> the <u>finest</u> ground beef" or "An electric mixer will combine the ingredients <u>quickly</u>, but don't use one. You should do this <u>by</u> hand." Always underline the grammar point that you have used so the teacher can see what you are trying to practice.

★Do not use just possessive adjectives (e.g., "your books") or numerical adjectives (e.g., "five books"). Use descriptive adjectives such as "a cold, windy evening" or "some old, faded T-shirts."

Unit 6

Prepositions after Verbs and Adjectives

1. VERB + PREPOSITION
2. ADJECTIVE + PREPOSITION

I'm really looking forward TO eating dinner at Gina's house tomorrow night.

Yes, so am I! You can always count ON Gina to cook something that is incredible.

VERB + PREPOSITION

Most verbs in English can be followed by a noun (or pronoun). These are called **transitive verbs.** Examples include **eat, write,** and **expect.**

	subject	+ VERB	+ object
examples:	The children	have eaten	all the candy.
	I	didn't write	two letters.
	Nobody	expected	such a hard test.

Other verbs cannot be followed by an object. These verbs are called **intransitive verbs.** Intransitive verbs require a preposition between the verb and the object.

Three common examples of intransitive verbs in English are **look, listen,** and **wait.** To make a sentence with **look** followed by an object, it is necessary to include the

83

preposition **at**. In English, you cannot **look something**. In English, you can only **look at something**. The verbs **listen** and **wait** are similar, but they require different prepositions.

Remember: **look AT** something, **listen TO** something, **wait FOR** someone

The verbs in this group are difficult for two reasons. First, in some languages, these verbs do not use any preposition. They are followed by an object and are therefore transitive. In English, however, these verbs are intransitive and must have a preposition.

The second difficulty for students is remembering which preposition goes with which verb. There are no rules to help you remember to say, "look AT" instead of "look BY" or "look ON." An excellent way to remember these verb and preposition combinations is to practice saying them aloud over and over. Pay attention to this in the speaking activities in this book. Some students also find it helpful to compare the preposition that English uses with the preposition that their language uses (if any) with that same verb.

VERB + PREPOSITION	*Example Sentences*
agree with	I **agree with** Bill.
approve of	Do you **approve of** the idea?
ask (someone) for	They **asked** me **for** my credit card expiration date.
belong to	The green car **belongs to** Amy.
complain about	Where can I **complain about** the cost of these tickets?
concentrate on	It was noisy in the room, so I couldn't **concentrate on** my homework.
consist of	The lunch special **consists of** one kind of meat and two vegetables.
count on	If she's your friend, then you can **count on** her.
depend on	For the past two years, I've **depended on** my dad for money.
forget about	Did you **forget about** the meeting tomorrow night?
give (something) to	When you are done with calculator, please **give** it **to** José.
happen to	What **happened to** Pablo?
listen to	He never **listens to** the teacher.
look at	Can you type without **looking at** the computer?
look for	I waste a lot of time just **looking for** my keys.
look forward to	Fran is really **looking forward** to the trip.
remind (someone) of	That song **reminds** me **of** my university days.
speak to	I **spoke to** Mike for a few minutes.
speak with★	You should **speak with** the doctor as soon as possible.
talk to	When did you **talk to** Melissa?
talk with★	It's important for you to **talk with** the doctor today.
thank (someone) for	She **thanked** her **for** the money.
think of	I'm trying to **think of** the best way to fix this broken pipe.
wait for	How long do you usually **wait for** the bus in the morning?
write to	Could you **write to** Jay and me?

★In these examples, **with** is used in a more formal or serious situation than **to.**

Exercise 1. Underline the correct pronoun. Follow the examples.

1. I agree (to, for, <u>with</u>) you on this topic.

2. Do you approve (<u>of</u>, with, at) her proposal?

3. Why did he ask me (with, for, on) my I.D.?

4. Whose green sweater is this? Who does it belong (by, for, to)?

5. The president is depending (to, with, on) getting votes from lots of young people.

6. The guest was complaining (about, for, with) the dirty towels.

7. When did you give the letters (for, at, to) your mom?

8. Look at your car! What happened (on, by, to) it?

9. Listen (at, for, to) me! You need to pay better attention in class.

10. I went to the beach to look (at, with, by) the waves crashing on the shore.

11. I'm really looking forward (by, since, to) my vacation next week.

12. You remind me (for, by, of) my old girlfriend.

13. I was lonely there. I didn't have anyone that I could talk (on, by, to).

14. Thank you (for, with, to) your time and help.

15. I heard about the bad news, so I'm trying to think (for, with, of) something good.

16. We waited (for, to, at) Bill for twenty minutes. We'll leave without him next time!

17. If you don't concentrate (in, on, to) your classes, you'll never learn English well.

18. How could you forget (for, in, about) Susan's birthday party? She was so disappointed that you didn't come.

Exercise 2. Circle the verb and then fill in the missing prepositions. Try to concentrate on the verb and preposition combinations.

1. We are (looking forward) ____to____ our trip next week. We want to thank you again _____ letting us use your apartment while we are in Los Angeles.

2. I was in the library all afternoon. I was looking _____ an article about a new computer technology. The quality of the paper that I have to write really depends a lot _____ whether or not I can find that article.

3. What a beautiful car! It reminds me a little _____ the first car
   I had. And I totally agree _____ you that red and green are
   the best colors for a new car. If I can think _____ a way to
   earn more money, I might get a new car next fall.

4. If you don't like the food at this hotel, you should complain _____ it by
   writing a letter to the company president. He is in charge of our budget, and that's
   what controls what we can or cannot serve. If you expect to see any changes, then I
   would suggest that you write _____ Mr. Will Miller, the company president. He
   is always interested in hearing from customers. He really listens _____ what
   they tell him. I don't think you'll have to wait very long _____ a response from
   him. He's usually extremely prompt.

ADJECTIVE + PREPOSITION

This list consists of frequently used adjectives and words functioning as adjectives and their
corresponding prepositions. Sometimes other prepositions are possible, too.

be + **ADJECTIVE** + **PREPOSITION**	*Example Sentences*
be accustomed to	I'm **accustomed to** eggs for breakfast.
be acquainted with	Are you **acquainted with** Picasso's works?
be afraid of	He's **afraid of** spiders.
be angry at	Why are you so **angry at** her?
be ashamed of	She's **ashamed of** what she did.
be aware of	We were not **aware of** any problems with the car.
be bad at	She's **bad at** tennis.
be bored with/by	I was **bored with** the play, so I left.
be composed of	Water is **composed of** hydrogen and oxygen.
be confused about	I'm so **confused about** this situation.
be convinced of	The government is **convinced of** the need to increase taxes.
be crazy about	Why are you so **crazy about** baseball?
be curious about	I'm **curious about** her past.
be different from	How is this paint **different from** that paint?
be disappointed in/with	We were **disappointed with** the food.
be done with	Are you **done with** the homework?
be envious of	I'm **envious of** your ability to sing.
be excited about	He's **excited about** going* on vacation next week.
be exhausted from	I was **exhausted from** the trip.
be familiar with	Are you **familiar with** this road?

be famous for	Switzerland is **famous for** its watches.
be finished with	Are you **finished with** the computer?
be far from	India is **far from** Canada.
be fed up with	I was **fed up with** the service at my bank, so I changed banks.
be full of	The car was **full of** suitcases.
be good at	Are you **good at** sports?
be guilty of	I think he is **guilty of** taking the money.
be happy about	Everyone was **happy about** the results of the game.
be harmful to	Smoking is **harmful to** everyone's health.
be impressed by/with	We were **impressed with** the service at the restaurant.
be innocent of	Do you think he is **innocent of** the crime?
be interested in	Are you **interested in** going to the beach with me?
be jealous of	I'm **jealous of** her! She's so lucky!
be known for	Korea is **known for** its spicy kim chee.
be made of/from	Mayonnaise is **made of** egg yolks and vegetable oil.
be married to	He was **married to** someone else when I first met him.
be opposed to	I'm **opposed to** eating at that restaurant again.
be polite to	He is always so **polite to** everyone.
be proud of	I'm so **proud of** my son's accomplishments.
be related to	Are you **related to** Donald Sibber?
be ready for	Are you **ready for** some dessert now?
be relevant to	That is not **relevant to** this topic.
be responsible for	You are **responsible for** your children's actions.
be satisfied with	Are you **satisfied with** the president's work so far?
be scared of	We aren't **scared of** anyone or anything.
be sick of	I'm **sick of** eating tuna fish sandwiches every day!
be similar to	Italian is **similar to** Spanish.
be sorry about	I'm **sorry about** spilling coffee on your shirt.
be successful in	He was very **successful in** the carpet industry.
be surprised at/by	No one was **surprised at** the election results.
be tired of	We are **tired of** eating chicken every day.
be tired from	We are **tired from** working in the yard today.
be used to	Kim and Hank are **used to** waking up early.
be worried about	We are not **worried about** arriving late.

*Note that if there is a verb after a preposition, the verb is in the gerund form. For more information, see Unit 9.

CAREFUL! Watch out for these common mistakes.

1. Do not use the wrong preposition with an adjective.
   wrong: She is similar for her sister.
   correct: She is similar to her sister.

2. Don't forget to use a form of the verb **to be** if necessary.
   wrong: She disappointed with the results of her test.
   correct: She was disappointed with the results of her test.

3. Don't confuse **used to + VERB** (past repeated actions) with **be + used to** (a habit or custom). **Be + used to + VERB + -ing** is the same as **be + accustomed to + VERB + -ing**.

wrong: We didn't eat hot dogs before coming here, but now we used to eat them.

correct: We didn't eat hot dogs before coming here, but now we're used to eating them.

Exercise 3. Matching. Underline the adjective in the phrases in the left column. Then connect the phrases in the right column with the correct beginning phrase in the left column. Write the letter of the correct ending on the line. Pay attention to the ADJECTIVE + PREPOSITION combinations. Follow the example.

__E__ 1. I've never been very <u>good</u>   A. about her great test score.

_____ 2. I don't know why you are so scared   B. from lifting boxes all day today.

_____ 3. Macaroni is similar   C. of eating tuna fish every day.

_____ 4. Of course she was happy   D. of snakes.

_____ 5. Alaska is known   E. at algebra.

_____ 6. Not again! I'm tired   F. to spaghetti.

_____ 7. My arms hurt. They're tired   G. for its scenery.

_____ 8. No one was very interested   H. in going on the trip.

Alaska

Exercise 4. Fill in the blank with the correct preposition. Use each one once.

in   at   to   from   with   for   about   of

1. Are you ready _____ the big exam tomorrow?

2. The museum is not so far _____ my house, so sometimes I walk there.

3. Jack was fed up _____ his neighbors' noise, so he called the police.

4. Mrs. Kim was so proud _____ her son when he won the essay contest.

5. It is well known that smoking is extremely harmful _____ human beings.

6. I heard that Gary has been very successful _____ his new position.

7. When she gets angry _____ someone, her face turns dark red.

8. I'm really sorry _____ spilling my soda on your carpet.

Exercise 5.   Grouping Activity. Write the adjectives from the list on pages 86–87 in the correct preposition group. Sometimes an adjective may be in more than one group. Follow the examples.

of

1. be _____afraid_____ of

2. be _____ of

3. be _____ of

4. be _____ of

5. be _____ of

6. be _____ of

7. be _____ of

8. be _____ of

9. be _____ of

10. be _____ of

11. be _____ of

12. be _____ of

13. be _____ of

14. be _____ of

15. be _____ of

to

1. be _____accustomed_____ to

2. be _____ to

3. be _____ to

4. be _____ to

5. be _____ to

6. be _____ to

7. be _____ to

8. be _____ to

9. be _____ to

with

1. be _____ with

2. be _____ with

3. be _____ with

4. be _____ with

5. be _____ with

6. be _____ with

7. be _____ with

8. be _____ with

9. be _____ with

at

1. be _____ at

2. be _____ at

3. be _____ at

4. be _____ at

about

1. be _____ about

2. be _____ about

3. be _____ about

4. be _____ about

5. be _____ about

6. be _____ about

7. be _____ about

for

1. be _____ for

2. be _____ for

3. be _____ for

4. be _____ for

Exercise 6. Write the correct prepositions on the lines. Follow the examples.

1. be confused	_about_	19. be convinced	_____	37. be harmful	_____
2. be disappointed	_in/with_	20. be aware	_____	38. be excited	_____
3. be bad	_____	21. be angry	_____	39. be happy	_____
4. be ashamed	_____	22. be exhausted	_____	40. be familiar	_____
5. be guilty	_____	23. be impressed	_____	41. be tired	_____
6. be proud	_____	24. be related	_____	42. be innocent	_____
7. be afraid	_____	25. be married	_____	43. be opposed	_____
8. be polite	_____	26. be finished	_____	44. be far	_____
9. be tired	_____	27. be ready	_____	45. be relevant	_____
10. be responsible	_____	28. be satisfied	_____	46. be scared	_____
11. be acquainted	_____	29. be done	_____	47. be envious	_____
12. be used	_____	30. be worried	_____	48. be fed up	_____
13. be interested	_____	31. be jealous	_____	49. be known	_____
14. be made	_____	32. be crazy	_____	50. be curious	_____
15. be different	_____	33. be famous	_____	51. be bored	_____
16. be composed	_____	34. be accustomed	_____	52. be full	_____
17. be good	_____	35. be sick	_____	53. be similar	_____
18. be sorry	_____	36. be successful	_____	54. be surprised	_____

Exercise 7. *Used To* vs. *Be Used To*. Fill in the blanks with the missing words. Sometimes you may have to use a negative. Follow the examples.

1. When I was a child, I ____used to____ hate onions, but now I love them.

2. When I was a child, I ___was used to___ waking up early in the morning, but I can't do that now.

3. I lived in Japan in 1994. When I left Japan, I _____ eating sushi.

4. When I lived in Japan, I _____ eat sushi once or twice a week.

5. Some people say that children _____ be more polite than they are now.

6. Driving in Canada is easy for me because I _____ driving on the right side of the road.

7. I don't like this new diet. I _____ eating so many green vegetables.

8. What a beautiful flower garden! When I was in junior high, I _____ have

   a flower garden, too.

CHALLENGE   An adult student wrote this sentence: "I was used to have a dog
when I was a kid, but it died." Is this sentence correct? If not, how would you change it?

Speaking Activity

Exercise 8.   Speaking Activity: Twenty Points

Step 1.   Choose any ten ADJECTIVE + PREPOSITION combinations from the list on
            pages 86–87. Write them in the first two columns below.

Step 2.   Work with a partner. Student A will call out one of the adjectives from the
            list on this page. Student B must respond with the correct preposition. A
            correct answer the first time gets two points and the second time one
            point. (No points are given for more than two tries.) Therefore, a perfect
            score would be twenty points. Write your partner's points in the column
            on the right. After A has asked B ten adjectives, then B can ask A ten
            adjectives.

> *example:*   A: "Number 1. Similar."
>   B: "Similar to."
>   A: Correct. Two points. Number 2. Good."
>   B: "Good in."
>   A: "No, that's not correct. Try again. Good."
>   B: "Good at."
>   A: "Yes, that's correct. One point. Now your total score is
>   three points. Number 3. Curious."

	Adjective	Preposition	Your Partner's Points
1.	_____	_____	_____
2.	_____	_____	_____
3.	_____	_____	_____
4.	_____	_____	_____
5.	_____	_____	_____
6.	_____	_____	_____
7.	_____	_____	_____
8.	_____	_____	_____
9.	_____	_____	_____
10.	_____	_____	_____

Speaking Activity

Exercise 9.   Speaking Activity: Pair Conversation

Step 1.   Work with a partner. Write an original conversation using six to ten of the ADJECTIVE + PREPOSITION combinations from the list on pages 86–87. Underline all of the ADJECTIVE + PREPOSITION combinations.

Step 2.   Make sure that both of your books are the same. When you finish, ask another student to check your work.

Step 3.   Present your conversation to the class. Both of you should stand at the front of the room and read your conversation. Speak clearly and be energetic when you perform. Be especially sure to pronounce the ADJECTIVE + PREPOSITION combinations loudly and clearly.

Before you read the conversation to your classmates, read just the adjectives that you have used and let other classmates tell you the prepositions. For example, if you used *jealous* in your conversation, say, "jealous" and wait until someone says, "jealous of."

A: _____

_____

B: _____

_____

A: _____

_____

B: _____

_____

A: _____

_____

B: _____

_____

A: _____

_____

B: _____

_____

A: _____

_____

B: _____

_____

Speaking Activity

Exercise 10a.   Speaking Activity: Crossword Puzzle, Student A

Two students work together. Use the clues on this page to fill in as many of the words as possible. Then take turns asking each other questions about the information that is missing from the puzzle. Student A works on the first crossword puzzle while student B works on the second crossword puzzle. Do NOT look at your partner's puzzle at any time.

Across

1. I don't know what to do in this situation. I'm so _____ about what to do!

5. She is Mrs. Smith. This means that she's _____ to Mr. Smith.

8. I'm angry _____ Sam for what he did.

10. the opposite of happy

15. the simple form of "done"

18. a dozen minus two

Down

1. A poem is _____ of words.

2. I needed a pencil, so I asked Jim _____ one.

4. not guilty of a crime

7. What happened to my car? Look at _____. Someone hit my car!

12. I can't do math. I'm _____ at it.

16. I don't approve _____ this plan.

Speaking Activity

Exercise 10b.   Speaking Activity: Crossword Puzzle, Student B

Two students work together. Use the clues on this page to fill in as many of the words as possible. Then take turns asking each other questions about the information that is missing from the puzzle. Student B works on the second crossword puzzle while student A works on the first crossword puzzle. Do NOT look at your partner's puzzle at any time.

Across

1. I wrote my answers in the wrong place. I was _____ about where to write them.

7. She is very successful _____ her business.

9. I'm really looking forward _____ seeing the basketball game tonight.

13. Are you _____ of any problems with this computer? I don't know of any.

17. past tense of 15 across

18. an even number between 7 and 11

19. We were so surprised _____ what she did.

Down

1. The UN Security Council is _____ of five permanent members.

3. If you're not feeling well, then you ought to _____ with your doctor.

6. Are you _____ for your big trip tomorrow? Have you packed?

11. This watch was _____ in Switzerland.

14. The past tense of this present tense form of a verb sounds like the number "one."

16. I'm tired _____ doing this work alone. Help me!

Exercise 11.   Multiple Choice. Circle the letter of the correct answer.

1. "Did you do a lot of things with your father when you were younger?"

   "Definitely. My dad and I _____ fishing a couple of times a month."

   (A) used to go   (C) used to going

   (B) were used to go   (D) were going to use

2. "What is the lunch special?"

   "Today's special consists _____ fried or baked chicken, a salad, and a vegetable."

   (A) in   (C) for

   (B) to   (D) of

3. "How do you have enough money to live? Your salary is pretty low."★

   "Actually, I depend _____ my parents for help."

   (A) with   (C) to

   (B) on   (D) in

4. "What do you think of her work?"

   "I'm _____ about her art. She's great!"

   (A) crazy   (C) envious

   (B) impressed   (D) proud

5. "Your trip is the day after tomorrow, isn't it?"

   "Yes, and I'm so excited _____ to Brazil."

   (A) for go   (C) for going

   (B) about go   (D) about going

6. "How was your vacation?"

   "We had a great time, but we're exhausted _____ being on the go for twenty

   days."

   (A) to   (C) from

   (B) for   (D) about

★This conversation deals with money, a topic that is considered personal. The two people in this conversation are probably very close friends.

7. "Why are you opposed _____ the new plan?"

    "I don't know. I don't like it at all."

    (A) for   (C) of

    (B) to   (D) about

8. "Who is _____ for what happened?"

    "I believe it's Mr. Wheeler."

    (A) accustomed   (C) envious

    (B) responsible   (D) fed up

Exercise 12.   Review Test

Part 1.   Read this short conversation. Fill in the blanks with the missing prepositions.

Barb: What happened _____ Maria?

Larry: She had a bike accident. She ran into another cyclist.

Barb: Is she OK?

Larry: She's going to be fine, but the bike is useless now.

Barb: Who did the bike belong _____?

Larry: It was hers. She bought it three days ago.

Barb: Her parents let her buy a bike?

Larry: They were opposed _____ her buying a new bike. Even though they

             didn't approve _____ her decision to buy a bike, they gave her some

             money to help pay for it.

Barb: So whose fault was the accident? Maria's or the other cyclist's?

Larry: Well, the answer depends _____ whose story you believe. Maria says

             that she was in the right, but the other cyclist claims that he didn't do any-

             thing wrong either.

Barb: I hope everything turns out OK. I know Maria's father must be very worried

             _____ her.

Part 2.   Read each sentence carefully. Look at the underlined part. If the underlined part is correct, circle the word *correct*. If it is wrong, circle the wrong
part and write the correct form above.

correct   wrong   1. Japanese rice is not similar <u>to</u> American rice.

correct   wrong   2. The teacher <u>was so fed up with</u> Jack's bad manners that she asked
him to leave the room.

correct   wrong   3. My grandfather <u>used to own</u> a small store on Greene Street.

correct   wrong   4. I don't think it's a good idea to <u>count with</u> your parents for help
now.

correct   wrong   5. In general, I agree <u>to</u> you that I was not polite to you. I'm sorry.

correct   wrong   6. That's a bad idea. <u>I'm very much opposed to buy</u> a new car now.

correct   wrong   7. Is this article relevant <u>to</u> the essay that you are writing for Dr.
Fender?

correct   wrong   8. I always have to <u>wait the bus</u> after school, and this is a waste of
time.

Extra Writing Practice

Situation: Write a dialogue in which two or three students are discussing
two of their classes. One class is the math class taught by Ms. Palacio and
the other is the English class taught by Mr. Ivone. The students are talking
about why they think each of the classes is good or bad. They are also
talking about each teacher's classroom policies.

Be sure to practice several VERB + PREPOSITION or ADJEC-
TIVE + PREPOSITION combinations that you have seen in this unit.
For example, one of the students might say, "You know, I'<u>m</u> not very
<u>good at</u> math, but I like Mr. Ivone's class, and I <u>look forward to</u> it every
day." Always underline the grammar point that you have used so the
teacher can see what you are trying to practice.

Unit 7

Passive Voice

1. form: *be* + PAST PARTICIPLE
2. usage
3. passive forms used as adjectives *(closed)*
4. passive forms (past participle) plus preposition
5. *-ing* vs. *-ed* adjectives (participial adjectives) *(interesting* vs. *interested)*

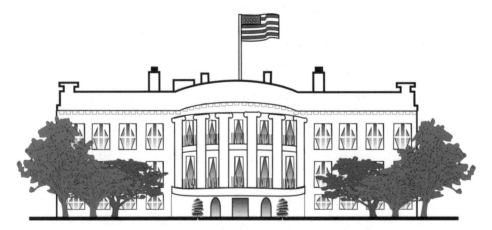

The residence of the president of the United States IS CALLED the White House.
The current White House WAS BUILT in 1818.
The original White House WAS DESTROYED in a fire in 1814.

	Active Voice	**Passive Voice**
	VERB	*be* + PAST PARTICIPLE
present	I **wash** my car every Saturday.	My car **is washed** every Saturday.
past	Shakespeare **wrote** that play.	That play **was written** by Shakespeare.
present progressive	They **are making** a special plan.	A special plan **is being made**.
be + going to	They**'re going to build** a house here.	A house **is going to be built** here.
modals	The government **should prohibit** the sale of cigarettes.	The sale of cigarettes **should be prohibited** by the government.

98

have to	We **have to clean** the house today.	The house **has to be cleaned** today.
past progressive	They **were** still **cooking** when the guests started to arrive.	The food **was** still **being cooked** when the guests started to arrive.
present perfect	People **have** officially **celebrated** Mother's Day since 1914.	Mother's Day **has** officially **been celebrated** since 1914.

Active Voice

A common sentence pattern in English is **subject + VERB + object.** In these sentences, the most important topic is the person or thing that is doing the action (the "doer" of the action). In these sentences, the subject is the doer of the action. This is called **active voice.** Can you identify the three parts (subject, verb, and object) in these example sentences?

     (A) The people of France gave the Statue of Liberty to the United States.
     (B) Leonardo da Vinci painted the famous *Mona Lisa.*
     (C) We will make a decision about our trip by tomorrow.
     (D) The people reelected George Washington for a second term in 1792.

In these four sentences with active voice, the emphasis is on **the people of France, Leonardo da Vinci, we,** and **the people.**

Passive Voice

Sentences in passive voice also begin with a subject and have a verb, but the subject here is *not* the doer of the action. In passive voice, the subject is the person or thing that "receives" the action of the verb. Here are the same four examples from above, but they are in passive voice. Can you see the differences?

     (A) The Statue of Liberty was given to the United States by the people of France.
     (B) The famous *Mona Lisa* was painted by Leonardo da Vinci.
     (C) A decision about our trip will be made by tomorrow.
     (D) George Washington was reelected for a second term in 1792.

In these sentences with passive voice, the emphasis is on **the Statue of Liberty, the famous** Mona Lisa, **a decision about our trip,** and **George Washington.**

Usage
In general, we use passive voice when the doer of the action is not the most important thing. In passive voice, the subject of the sentence is the receiver of the action. The subject can be either a person or a thing.

If you want to name the doer in a passive voice sentence, you can use a **by** + **doer** phrase. You can see this in examples (A) and (B). However, sometimes it sounds strange to name the doer. You should not name the doer when it is not new information. For example, in (D), we know that every president is elected by the people, so it is not usual to say, "President Washington was reelected by the people for a second term in 1792." The phrase **by the people** does not tell us any new or important information.

Passive voice is more common in written language than in spoken language, but it occurs in both. Passive voice is more common in formal, planned language than it is in informal, ordinary conversations, but it can occur in all of these situations.

Form

The passive voice is composed of the verb **be** and the past participle. The verb **be** should be in the correct tense to indicate the time of the action. In addition, it should also be singular or plural according to the number of the subject.

When you change a verb from active voice to passive voice, a helpful hint is to count the number of verb parts in the active sentence and then add one. The number of verb parts in the passive sentence is always one more than the number of verb parts in the active sentence. This is due to the addition of a form of the verb **be** to the passive sentence.

Pay attention to the number of verb parts in these active and passive sentences.

Active	*Passive*

People <u>write</u> Arabic from right to left.
      1
	Arabic <u>is written</u> from right to left.
	   1 **2**

The vice president <u>will</u> <u>lead</u> the meeting.
           1   **2**
	The meeting <u>will</u> <u>be</u> <u>led</u> by the vice president.
	           1 **2** **3**

Local artists <u>are</u> <u>going</u> <u>to</u> <u>do</u> the paintings.
        1 **2** **3** **4**
	The paintings <u>are</u> <u>going</u> <u>to</u> <u>be</u> <u>done</u> by local artists.
	         1 **2** **3** **4** **5**

CAREFUL! Do not make these common mistakes.

1. Do not use active voice when you should use passive voice.
   wrong: The final exam will give on May 19th.
   correct: The final exam will be given on May 19th.

   unusual: The man bit the dog. (grammatically possible but not probable!)
   correct: The man was bitten by the dog.

2. Do not forget to use a form of **be** in the passive voice.
   wrong: This letter sent to the wrong address.
   correct: This letter was sent to the wrong address.

wrong: I don't have my car today. It's fixed.
correct: I don't have my car today. It's being fixed.

3. Do not use the **by + doer** phrase if the information is not new or important.
    unusual: President Clinton was elected by the people in 1992.
    usual: President Clinton was elected in 1992.

    unusual: When red and white paints are mixed by someone, the result is pink
                  paint.
    usual: When red and white paints are mixed, the result is pink paint.

4. Some verbs can *never* be in passive voice. These verbs★ do not have an object in
    active voice, so they cannot be changed to passive voice. Examples of verbs that
    are never used in passive voice are **happen, die, arrive, exit, depart** (many
    verbs of motion).
    wrong: The accident was happened late last night.
    correct: The accident happened late last night.

    wrong: Five people were died in the plane crash.
    correct: Five people died in the plane crash.

    wrong: When we were arrived at the party, it began to rain heavily.
    correct: When we arrived at the party, it began to rain heavily.

★These verbs are called **intransitive verbs.** See unit 6, pages 83–84, for more information.

Exercise 1.   Fill in the correct passive voice forms for the active voice phrase.
                   Follow the example.

	Active Voice	*Passive Voice*
present tense	People do X.	X ____is done____
present progressive tense	People are doing X.	X _____
past tense	People did X.	X _____
modals	People should do X.	X _____
	People might do X.	X _____
have to	People have to do X.	X _____
be + going to	People are going to do X.	X _____
past progressive tense	People were doing X.	X _____
present perfect tense	People have done X.	X _____

Exercise 2.   Fill in the blanks with the correct active or passive voice forms.
                    Follow the example.

Active   *Passive*

1. Bell <u>invented</u> the telephone in 1876.   The telephone ___was invented___

                                                      by Bell in 1876.

2. Native speakers <u>write</u> English from left to   English _____ from left

   right.   to right.

3. When _____ doctors _____ a   When <u>will</u> a cure for AIDS <u>be found</u>?

   cure for AIDS?

4. The owners <u>have sold</u> the historic hotel   The historic hotel _____

   to a group of buyers from Japan.   to a group of buyers from Japan.

5. Of course you <u>should take</u> a practice test   Of course a practice test _____

   before taking the real TOEFL.   before taking the real TOEFL.

6. We _____ all of the   All of the work <u>is going to be finished</u> by

   work by 4 P.M.   4 P.M.

7. We _____ all of the   All of the work <u>was finished</u> by 4 P.M.

   work by 4 P.M.

8. OK, we <u>have finished</u> all of the work.   All of the work _____.

   Now we can go home.   Now we can go home.

9. They _____ lunch   Lunch <u>was being cooked</u> when

   when the fire started.   the fire started.

10. We <u>built</u> this house in 1952.   This house _____ in

                                                      1952.

Exercise 3.   Underline the correct verb forms. Follow the example.

1. If blue paint (mixes, <u>is mixed</u>) with yellow paint, what color paint do you get?

2. The taxi driver (took, was taken) the tourists from the airport to their hotel.

3. Temperature in the United States (measures, is measured) with the Fahrenheit scale.

4. Fresh fish can (fry or bake, be fried or baked). It can (serve, be served) with french
   fries or a baked potato.

5. If you (take, are taken) photos in the shade, they might not look so good.

6. The current White House (builds, is built, built, was built) in 1818.

7. Peter (fired, was fired) because he (didn't attend, wasn't attended) the training session.

8. In Japan, people (eat, are eaten) rice with nothing on it. However, in the U.S. and Canada, rice usually (eats, ate, is eating, is eaten) with some kind of meat or gravy.

9. He (learned, was learned) all the vocabulary by writing each word five times.

10. The driver's license exam (gives, is giving, is given) every Tuesday and Friday morning.

Exercise 4. Fill in the blanks in this job advertisement with the correct forms of the verbs in parentheses. Follow the example.

Wanted: Spanish Instructor

Jamestown High School (look) _____is looking_____ for a Spanish instructor for upcoming fall classes. The ideal candidate (teach) _____ Spanish for at least three years. The top candidates will (interview) _____ by school administrators at the job fair at the University of Rutford next week. Resumes should (send) _____ to Rita Williams at Jamestown High School, 4718 Thomas Street, Jamestown, FL 33410. Successful applicants will (call) _____ before the job fair.

Exercise 5. Matching. Form correct sentences by writing the letters of the items in the right column on the lines in the left column. In some cases there are several possible combinations, but choose the combinations that will produce ten sentences that are good in both grammar and meaning. Follow the example.

  J   1. Most of the books on the bottom shelf   A. was explained in thirty minutes.

_____ 2. The knives   B. has to cut up the onions.

_____ 3. First, the onions   C. write true stories.

_____ 4. First, the cook   D. explained the lesson carefully.

_____ 5. Really interesting authors   E. must be cut up.

_____ 6. The irregular verbs   F. must be learned by heart.

_____ 7. The serious students in the class   G. learned the list by heart.

_____ 8. The instructor   H. should be put in this drawer.

_____ 9. The easy computer program   I. are written from real experience.

_____10. The best stories   J. were written in the early 1800s.

Exercise 6.   Editing. Read each sentence carefully. Look at the underlined part. If the underlined part is correct, circle the word *correct*. If it is wrong, circle the wrong part and write the correct form above. Follow the example.

(correct) wrong   1. One of the most popular cars in the U.S. <u>is made</u> in Japan.

correct wrong   2. From a total of fifty people, Jason <u>was chosen</u> the best chef.

correct wrong   3. The weight of a passenger's suitcases <u>limited</u> to 44 pounds.

correct wrong   4. When her grandfather <u>was died</u>, she was extremely upset.

correct wrong   5. All of the work <u>has done</u>, so we can go home now.

correct wrong   6. Thousands of people went to California in the 1840s because gold <u>discovered</u> there.

correct wrong   7. When 4 <u>is multiplied</u> by 7, the product is 28.

correct wrong   8. I turned on the switch, but nothing <u>was happened</u>.

correct wrong   9. French <u>is spoken</u> by most of the people in Quebec.

correct wrong 10. On my last exam, the teacher <u>was marked</u> all the errors in bright red.

correct wrong 11. This beautiful house was constructed <u>by builders</u> in the 1920s.

correct wrong 12. This beautiful house was constructed <u>by my uncle</u> in the 1920s.

 Why is it that verbs like **die** (number 4) and **happen** (number 8) can never have a passive voice form?

Passive Forms Used as Adjectives

Sometimes it is possible to use a passive verb form as an adjective to describe a condition or state instead of an action. In this case, we use a past participle after a form of the verb **be.**

Sentence	*Notes*
The window **is closed.**	There is no action. This sentence describes the condition of the window now.
All of the checks **are gone.**	There is no action. This sentence describes the condition of the checks now.
The dinner **is cooked.** Let's eat.	There is no action. No one is cooking now. This sentence describes the condition of the dinner now.

Exercise 7. Write the passive form of the verbs in parentheses.

1. I don't like to shop on Saturday because the stores (crowd) _____.

2. I (interest) _____ in learning how to play golf.

3. Why (turn) _____ the light in this room _____ on?

4. When all of these envelopes (seal) _____, you can go home.

5. I think dinner (do) _____. Let's eat.

6. Can you tell me where the embassy is? I think I (lose) _____.

7. *Ann:* Do you have a family?

   Lynn: Yes, I (marry) _____. We have a baby girl.

8. *Amy:* I'm hungry. I think I'll cook some fish.

   Ben: You can't do that now. The fish (freeze) _____.

9. *Joe:* Are you from California originally?

   Tim: Actually, no. I (bear)★ _____ in Alaska.

★The verb *bear* means to produce something. We can use bear in active voice for animals and things. For example, we can say, "Cats often bear as many as five kittens" and "This kind of apple tree usually bears large apples in late August." It is rare to use this verb in the active voice with people. However, in passive voice we can say, "I was born in Texas" or "Both my parents were born in 1950."

10. *Jay:*   What's wrong with the switch?

    Pete: I don't know. It (stick) _____, and I can't get it to move.

11. *Mike:*   This lamp won't work now.

    Henry: Are you sure that it (plug) _____ in?

12. *Bob:*   Where is Kuala Lumpur?

    Ken: Kuala Lumpur (locate) _____ in Malaysia.

PAST PARTICIPLE + PREPOSITION

Here is a list of past participles that are similar to passive voice. You need to learn these combinations of **be** + **PAST PARTICIPLE** + **PREPOSITION**. (See pp. 86–87, Unit 6, for more information.)

be accustomed to	I'm **accustomed to** eating★ eggs for breakfast.
be acquainted with	Are you **acquainted with** Picasso's works?
be ashamed of	She's **ashamed of** what she did.
be bored with/by	I was **bored with** the game, so I left.
be committed to	Is the senator really **committed to** the new educational program?
be composed of	Water is **composed of** hydrogen and oxygen.
be confused about	I'm so **confused about** this situation.
be convinced of	The governor is **convinced of** the need to increase taxes.
be dedicated to	Professor Brown is certainly **dedicated to** her job.
be devoted to	That singer is **devoted to** his fans.
be disappointed in/with	We were **disappointed with** the food.
be divorced from	I'm **divorced from** her now.
be done with	Are you **done with** the homework?
be dressed in	What was he **dressed in**?
be excited about	He's **excited about** going★ on vacation next week.
be exhausted from	I was **exhausted from** the trip.
be finished with	Are you **finished with** the computer?
be fed up with	I was **fed up with** the service at my bank, so I changed banks.
be impressed by/with	We were **impressed with** the service at the restaurant.
be interested in	Are you **interested in** going★ to the beach with me?
be known for	Greece is **known for** its ancient temples.
be made of/from	Mayonnaise is **made of** egg yolks and vegetable oil.
be married to	She was **married to** someone else when I first met her.
be opposed to	I'm **opposed to** eating★ at that restaurant again.
be related to	Are you **related to** Marcia Brady?
be satisfied with	Are you **satisfied with** the new employee's work so far?

be scared of	We aren't **scared of** anyone or anything.
be surprised at/by	No one was **surprised at** the election results.
be terrified of	Since I was a small child, I have been **terrified of** mice.
be tired of	We are **tired of** eating★ peanut butter sandwiches every day.
be tired from	We are **tired from** working in the yard today.
be used to	Kim and Hank are **used to** waking★ up early.
be worried about	We are not **worried about** your grades.

★If there is a verb after a preposition, note that the verb is in the gerund form.

Exercise 8.   Fill in the blanks with the correct phrase. Be sure to include the verb *be,* the past participle, and the preposition. Follow the example.

1. (oppose)   I ____ *am opposed to* ____ more construction in this area.

2. (excite)   Of course he _____ the great news when he heard it.

3. (know)   France _____ its cheeses.

4. (tire)   Hot dogs again! I _____ eating hot dogs every day!

5. (not relate)   Susan may look like Sarah, but she _____ her.

6. (ashamed)   I can't believe you told her that! You should _____

what you have done.

7. (scare)   I _____ all kinds of snakes.

8. (satisfy)   _____ you _____ the way they fixed your car?

9. (not do)   You look upset. You must _____ that history paper yet.

10. (confuse)   Sam wants the teacher to repeat the assignment. He _____

the exact assignment.

11. (acquaint)   _____ you _____ Hemingway's novels and stories?

12. (worry)   I've never seen you this nervous. What _____ you _____?

13. (compose)   A good sentence _____ a subject, a verb, and

additional information.

14. (tire)   At first, she said she would go shopping with me today, but now she says

she _____ working the garden all morning, so she

doesn't want to go shopping.

15. (exhaust)   At the end of the day, I _____ totally _____ washing

the car, mowing the lawn, and washing the clothes.

Speaking Activity

Exercise 9.   Speaking Activity: Practice with Passive Voice. What has been done?

Situation: Today is a big housework day. You have a list of things that you will definitely do today. Right now you are in the middle of the list of housework items. Some of these things have already been done, but the others haven't been done yet. However, by the end of the day, all of these chores will have been done.

Step 1.   There are twelve activities below. Put a check mark (√) by any four of the activities. Do this in the left "Your List" column. These are the four items that have been done already.

Step 2.   Next, work with a partner. Do NOT show your book to your partner. Take turns asking each other questions. Use passive voice in every question. Ask, "Has/have (chore) been done?" or "Has/Have (item) been (past participle)?" Your partner will answer either, "Yes, (the chore) has <u>already</u> been done" or "No, (the chore) hasn't been done <u>yet</u>." If the answer is YES, then you continue asking questions. If the answer is NO, then it is your partner's turn. Use passive voice in your questions and the words *already* or *yet* in your answers. Use complete sentences in your answers. Use the right "Your Partner's List" column to record which chores you have already asked about.

examples: A: Have the shirts been ironed?
             B: No, the shirts haven't been ironed yet. (The answer is NO, so A writes NO by "iron the shirts" in the column on the right. The NO answer also means that it is B's turn to ask a question.)
             B: Has the car been washed?
             A: Yes, the car has already been washed. (The answer is YES, so B writes YES by "wash the car" in the column on the right. The YES answer also means that it is still A's turn to ask a question.)

The winner is the first student who can guess all four of his or her partner's answers.

Your List

____ iron the shirts   ____ vacuum the carpet

____ take out the garbage   ____ wash the car

____ make the beds   ____ clean the bathroom

____ do the dishes   ____ cut the grass

____ mop the floors   ____ pay the bills

____ do the laundry   ____ water the flowers

Your Partner's List

___ iron the shirts	___ vacuum the carpet
___ take out the garbage	___ wash the car
___ make the beds	___ clean the bathroom
___ do the dishes	___ cut the grass
___ mop the floors	___ pay the bills
___ do the laundry	___ water the flowers

-ing vs. *-ed* Adjectives
(participial adjectives⋆)

We have already seen that the past participle of a verb can function as an adjective.

> *example:*   When I heard the news yesterday, I was **surprised**.

Sometimes the present participle of a verb can also function as an adjective.

> *example:*   The news was **surprising**.

–ing is for the person or thing that makes (causes) the action.
-ed (or any past participle ending) is for the person or thing that receives the action.

⋆The *-ing* adjective is a present participle. The *-ed* adjective is a past participle.

	The news surprised me.	**Joe disappointed us.**
ACTION	surprise	disappoint
Person or thing that causes the action	the news = The news was surpris<u>ing</u>.	Joe = Joe was disappoint<u>ing</u>.
person or thing that receives the action	me = I was surpris<u>ed</u>.	us = We were disappoint<u>ed</u>.

Like other descriptive adjectives, the *-ing* and *-ed* (past participle) adjectives can come directly before a noun.

> *examples:*   The most <u>surprising</u> thing was the <u>bored</u> look on the
> students' faces.
> An <u>overbooked</u> flight can be a very <u>annoying</u> situation.
> By putting <u>frozen</u> fish and some sauce in the microwave oven,
> she created an <u>interesting</u> but quick dinner.

Common *-ing/-ed* (or participial) Adjectives

annoying	annoyed	exciting	excited
amazing	amazed	exhausting	exhausted
amusing	amused	fascinating	fascinated
astonishing	astonished	frightening	frightened
boring	bored	horrifying	horrified
confusing	confused	interesting	interested
convincing	convinced	puzzling	puzzled
depressing	depressed	satisfying	satisfied
disappointing	disappointed	shocking	shocked
disgusting	disgusted	startling	startled
embarrassing	embarrassed	terrifying	terrified
entertaining	entertained	tiring	tired

CAREFUL! Do not make these common mistakes.

1. Do not mix up when to use **-ing** and when to use **-ed** (past participle). They are completely different.

    wrong: What is that annoyed sound?
    correct: What is that annoying sound?

    wrong: I'm boring in that class. (possible, but the meaning is different)
    correct: I'm bored in that class.

2. Do not forget to use an ending. Do not use just the simple verb form as an adjective.

    wrong: The surprise results were on the front page of the paper.
    correct: The surprising results were on the front page of the paper.

Exercise 10.   Write the correct adjective form on the lines. Follow the examples.

1. The movie that Jill saw last night shocked her.

    (A) Jill was _____shocked_____.

    (B) The movie was really _____shocking_____.

    (C) Some of the scenes at the end of the movie were especially

    _____.

2. Patty's decision surprised everyone in the room.

    (A) Her decision was _____.

    (B) Everyone in the room was _____.

3. Question number five on the test perplexed Bob.

   (A) Bob had a _____ look on his face.

   (B) Question number five was _____.

   (C) Bob was _____.

4. That was the worst movie I've ever seen. It really disgusted me!

   (A) I was _____.

   (B) The whole movie was _____.

   (C) I'm sure that other people in the audience were _____, too.

   (D) The opening scene in which the soldiers were killed was too

   _____.

   (E) One audience member said, "What a _____ movie!"

5. Today's lesson confused all of the students.

   (A) The lesson was _____.

   (B) The teacher's explanations were _____.

   (C) The students were _____.

   (D) The _____ students are angry about the teacher's

   _____ explanations.

Exercise 11.   Underline the correct adjective form.

1. *Ann:*   I don't know what to do now. I'm so (1) (<u>confused</u>, confusing).

   Jack: Maybe you should talk to your mom. She knows you're having some

   problems, and I'm sure she's very (2) (interested, interesting) in hearing your

   problems.

2. *Zina:*   That book sounds (3) (interested, interesting).

   Carol: I like the part when the people were trapped in the car in the river. They

   were (4) (terrified, terrifying).

   Zina: Well, it sounds like a (5) (fascinated, fascinating) book. I'll get a copy as soon

   as I can.

3. *Paul:*   What are you doing this weekend?

   Alan: I'm driving to Miami.

   Paul: What do you mean?

   Alan: Why do you look so (6) (puzzled, puzzling)?

   Paul: Well, that's a really (7) (tired, tiring) trip. Why are you going there?

   Alan: I've been feeling sort of (8) (depressed, depressing) lately, so I've decided to do something totally different this weekend. One of my old college friends lives there, so I'm going to go visit him and his family. It'll be something different for sure.

   Paul: Hey, what's up? If you need anyone to talk to, just let me know. Some people are (9) (embarrassed, embarrassing) to talk to their friends about things, but please just let me know if there's anything I can do for you.

4. *Danny:*   Did you know that Susan has an (10) (amazed, amazing) stamp collection?

   Linda: No, I didn't. I didn't know she was (11) (interested, interesting) in stamp collecting.

   Danny: I didn't know it either, but you ought to see her collection.

   Linda: A stamp collection? You think that is (12) (interested, interesting)?

   Danny: Look. I was a little (13) (puzzled, puzzling) when I first heard that she had a stamp collection, but, Linda, it's not just a stamp collection.

   Linda: What do you mean?

   Danny: She has over 9,000 stamps! Some of them have quite (14) (fascinated, fascinating) stories behind them. For example, she has a stamp that was issued in Britain in 1800. Can you imagine?

   Linda: I thought looking at some stamps would be (15) (bored, boring), but I guess I'm wrong.

Exercise 12. Multiple Choice. Circle the letter of the correct answer.

1. "How was the restaurant last night? Was the food good?"

   "My salmon _____ enough, so I had to send it back to the kitchen."

   (A) wasn't cooked   (C) hasn't been cooked

   (B) wasn't been cooked   (D) isn't cooking

2. "Are you ready to go home now?"

   "Yes, I am. These letters _____ tomorrow morning, but I have to put stamps on

   them first."

   (A) have to be sent   (C) are sending

   (B) must send   (D) have been sent

3. "I can't believe I failed the driver's license test again."

   "I know you must be _____. However, you have to keep on trying!"

   (A) disappointing   (C) disappointed

   (B) disappoint   (D) have disappointed

4. In some countries, food _____ with the right hand instead of fork and spoon.

   (A) eats   (C) has been eaten

   (B) is eating   (D) is eaten

5. The large yellow house on the corner was _____.

   (A) built in 1957 by people   (C) built by people

   (B) built in 1957   (D) built by people in 1957

6. "What does this symbol on this toy mean?"

   "Toys with that symbol _____ especially for very young children."

   (A) are designing   (C) are designed

   (B) designed   (D) should design

7. When the announcer raised his arm, he split his shirt. Of course people in the

   audience were totally _____ incident.

   (A) surprising at this amused (C) surprising at this amusing

   (B) surprised at this amusing (D) surprised at this amused

8. "Have you ever been to New York?"

"Yes, in 1995. My wife and I _____ there in the fall. The weather was so nice then."

(A) were traveled   (C) traveled

(B) have traveled   (D) have been traveled

Exercise 13.   Review Test

Part 1.   Fill in the blanks with the passive voice of these verbs. (Some of these verbs may be used more than once; some verbs may not be used at all.) Be careful with the verb tenses.

choose	finish	cook	purchase	do
make	pack	worry	discover	take

1. *Joe:*   Are you ready for your trip tomorrow?

   Ben: Yes, I am. All of the plans _____.

   Joe: What about your air ticket? And the hotel reservations?

   Ben: The ticket _____ and the hotel reservations _____.

   Joe: Yes, you are ready! But what about your suitcases?

   Ben: Yep, both of my suitcases _____. I'm really ready to go!

2. *Amy:*   I'm so hungry.

   Mom: Dinner _____ almost _____. As soon as the potatoes _____, we can eat.

3. *Antonio:* I _____ about this test tomorrow. Ask me some more questions.

   Maria: OK. When _____ gold _____ in California?

Antonio: I think it was in the 1840s.

Maria: OK. When _____ Alaska _____ from Russia?

Antonio: I don't know. Ask me an easier question.

Maria: OK. The answer is 1867. Alaska was purchased from Russia in 1867.

     Next question. Who _____ president in 1900?

Part 2.   Read each sentence carefully. Look at the underlined part. If the under-lined part is correct, circle the word *correct.* If it is wrong, circle the wrong part and write the correct form above.

correct   wrong   1. My car was purchased in 1997 <u>by me</u>.

correct   wrong   2. All of the doors <u>has been locked</u>, so we can leave now.

correct   wrong   3. These beautiful stamps <u>printed</u> in East Germany in the 1970s.

correct   wrong   4. Where were you when the accident <u>was happened</u>?

correct   wrong   5. The fire that destroyed the apartment happened when dinner <u>was being cooked</u>.

correct   wrong   6. Over one hundred people <u>were killed</u> in that plane crash.

correct   wrong   7. When <u>was the U.S. Capitol built</u>?

correct   wrong   8. If you find a wallet, it <u>should be returning</u> to the owner immediately.

correct   wrong   9. To make stew for four people, you <u>should get</u> two pounds of meat.

correct   wrong   10. Japanese <u>can be written</u> from left to right or from top to bottom.

Extra Writing Practice

Situation: You are a real estate agent. Last week Mr. and Mrs. Taylor called you up and hired you as their agent to sell their home. As a real estate agent, you also have several people who have hired you because they want to buy a house. Your job is to persuade one of these buyers to purchase the Taylors' house. Write a paragraph in which you describe the house. You can make up any information that you want.

     Be sure to practice passive voice in your paragraph. For example, you might write, "This house <u>was built</u> in 1995" or "The house <u>was constructed</u> by skilled builders." Always underline the grammar point that you have used so the teacher can see what you are trying to practice.

Unit 8

Relative Clauses

1. *who, that, which*
2. subject position
3. object position *(whom)*
4. *whose*
5. Optional words: subject + *be*

Is this the new chair YOU BOUGHT last Saturday?

No, the chair THAT I BOUGHT is over here.

Discover Grammar

Each of these sentences is the result of combining two smaller sentences. Put one line under the main sentence. Then put parentheses around the extra part. Then write the two original sentences. Follow the example. Work with a partner if you want.

1. <u>The boy</u> (who is wearing a striped shirt) <u>is 12 years old.</u>

   Main sentence: _____The boy is 12 years old._____

   Extra sentence: _____The boy is wearing a striped shirt._____

2. We came here on a jet that can carry over 400 people.

   Main sentence: _____

   Extra sentence: _____

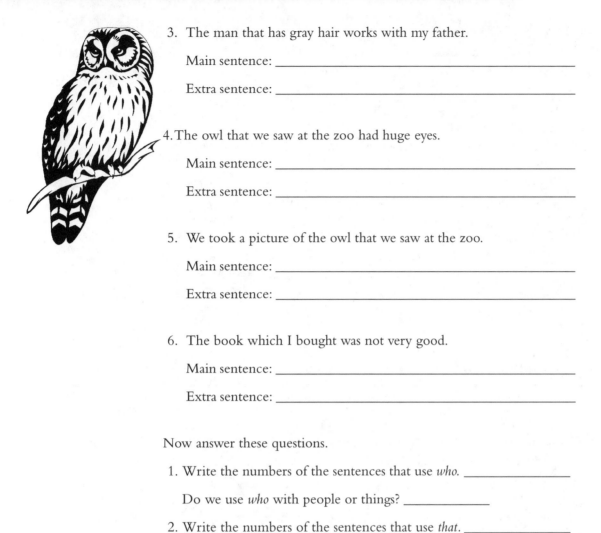

3. The man that has gray hair works with my father.

Main sentence: _____

Extra sentence: _____

4. The owl that we saw at the zoo had huge eyes.

Main sentence: _____

Extra sentence: _____

5. We took a picture of the owl that we saw at the zoo.

Main sentence: _____

Extra sentence: _____

6. The book which I bought was not very good.

Main sentence: _____

Extra sentence: _____

Now answer these questions.

1. Write the numbers of the sentences that use *who*. _____

   Do we use *who* with people or things? _____

2. Write the numbers of the sentences that use *that*. _____

   Do we use *that* with people or things? _____

3. Write the numbers of the sentences that use *which*. _____

   Do we use *which* with people or things? _____

[Check p. 134 for the answers.]

Grammar Notes for Relative Clauses

1. What is a relative clause?
   A clause is a group of words with a subject and a verb. A relative clause is a clause that describes or gives more information about a noun. A relative clause usually begins with **who, that, which, whom,** or **whose** (but sometimes **that, which,** and **whom** are omitted).

2. What does a relative clause look like? What are examples of relative clauses?

The parts <u>that are underlined</u> are relative clauses.

The man <u>who has gray hair</u> is my father.

We live near the stadium <u>that is on State Street</u>.

I did not enjoy the book <u>which Sue gave me for my birthday</u>.

The man <u>whom you met yesterday</u> works with my mother.

That is the man <u>whose son won the art contest</u>.

3. Where do relative clauses occur in a sentence?

Relative clauses may occur in the middle or at the end of a sentence. However, relative clauses are always placed very near the noun that they are describing.

wrong: The woman is a good teacher <u>that is standing by the door</u>.

correct: The woman <u>that is standing by the door</u> is a good teacher.

(Explanation: **Woman** is more general than **a good teacher.** You need to tell which woman is a good teacher, so the relative clause must go after **the woman**, not **a good teacher.**)

4. Are relative clauses common in English?

Yes, relative clauses are very common in English. They are used frequently in both writing and speaking, so it is important to be able to use them quickly and easily.

5. When do we use relative clauses in English?

We use relative clauses when we want to identify a noun or give more information about a noun. A relative clause in a sentence is really a new sentence that is being put inside of the main sentence.

6. What are the steps in creating a relative clause in English?

Step 1.   Find the word that is the same in both sentences.

Step 2.   Change the word to the correct relative pronoun or adjective **(who, that, which, whom, whose).**

Step 3.   Put the relative clause near the noun that is being described.

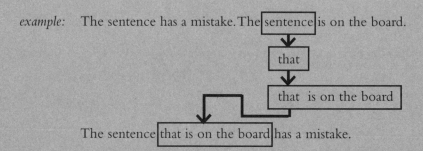

example: The sentence has a mistake. The sentence is on the board.

that

that is on the board

The sentence that is on the board has a mistake.

7. When do you use **who, that,** and **which?**

Use **who** for people. Use **which** for things. Use **that** for people or things.

This is the book <u>that I like</u>. This is the book <u>which I like</u>.

The woman <u>who drives a BMW</u> is Ms. Lim. The woman <u>that drives a BMW</u> is Ms. Lim.

CAREFUL! Watch out for these common mistakes.

1. Do not use the wrong word to begin a relative clause. Do not use **which** for people or **who** for things in relative clauses.
   wrong: The student which made 100 on the test is from China.
   correct: The student who made 100 on the test is from China.
   correct: The student that made 100 on the test is from China.

2. Do not put the relative clause in the wrong place. Keep it near the noun that is being described.
   (*situation:* You received a letter. I put it on the table. The letter is on the table now.)
   wrong: I put the letter on the table that you received. (This means you received the table, not the letter.)
   correct: I put the letter that you received on the table.

3. Do not forget to use a relative pronoun **(who, that, which).**
   wrong: The book has 250 pages is on the table.
   correct: The book that has 250 pages is on the table.
   correct: The book which has 250 pages is on the table.

Exercise 1. Underline the relative clauses in these sentences. Follow the example.

1. We decided to buy the same kind of car <u>that Joseph has</u>.

2. The car which we bought about seven years ago is not in good condition.

3. People who have children need a lot of patience.

4. Gold is a metal that has always been very valuable.

5. The number of people who live in Florida has increased every year since the 1960s.

6. We bought some cookies, but we didn't buy any of the cookies that had raisins in them.

Exercise 2. Underline the correct relative pronoun. Follow the example. Sometimes more than one answer is possible.

1. *Tomas:* Excuse me, but would you mind if I used your phone?

   Natasha: Sure, go ahead. You can use the phone (that, <u>which</u>, who) is in the kitchen.

2. *John:* Where are the books (that, which, who) we used yesterday?

   Mark: I don't know. You should ask the students (that, which, who) used them last.

3. *Carl:*   Is the class (that, which, who) you are taking now hard?

   Mike: Well, I like the professor (that, which, who) is teaching the course, but the

               course material is tough. In fact, the lesson (that, which, who) we are

               studying now is really tough.

4. *Greg:*   Hey, what's the name of the TV show (that, which, who) comes on after

               the news?

   Vicki: I don't know. I can ask my friend Lisa if you want. She is the kind of

               person (that, which, who) knows everything about TV and movies.

5. *Liz:*   Do you want to get some coffee somewhere?

   Ali: Yes, let's go to that new shop (that, which, who) is on the corner of 4th

               and Elm.

   Liz: OK. That sounds good to me. My friend told me that the coffee (that,

               which, who) they make there is incredible.

Relative Clauses: *that/who/which* as Subject

> *example:*   The man that is standing by the door works at the university.

This sentence is composed of two clauses. In other words, there are two subjects and two verbs. One clause provides the main information, and the other clause gives extra information.

The main verb in the sentence that you just analyzed is **works,** and the subject is **the man.** The second verb is **is standing,** and the subject is **that.** The analysis looks like this.

The man (that is standing by the door) works at the university.
Subject 1 Subject 2 Verb 2   Verb 1

Important: Notice the word **that** here is the subject of a verb. If a word is the subject, it is necessary. It cannot be omitted in any case at all.

SUMMARY: who, that, which as subject

	People	*Things*
	1. who	1. which
	2. that	2. that

examples:	1. I know the boy <u>who</u> won the spelling bee.	1. The book <u>which</u> is on the table has 200 pages.
	2. I know the boy <u>that</u> won the spelling bee.	2. The book <u>that</u> is on the table has 200 pages.

Exercise 3.   Each sentence has two clauses: a main clause and a relative clause.
              Put parentheses around the relative clause. Put one line under the
              subject of each clause; label these S1 and S2. Then put two lines
              under the verb in each clause; label these V1 and V2. Follow the
              example.

1. Our history <u>teacher</u> usually <u>gives</u> tests (<u>that</u> <u>have</u> multiple choice questions).
                     S1   V1   S2   V2

2. Tests that have multiple choice questions are not so difficult.

3. Drinking milk which doesn't have any fat in it is healthier than drinking regular milk.

4. I just can't stand the taste of milk which doesn't have any fat in it.

5. The man who won the marathon is from Kenya.

6. Everyone took photos of the man who won the marathon.

Exercise 4.   Read the two sentences and then complete the new sentence.
              Follow the example.

1. The woman wrote a popular novel. The woman came to our university last week.

    The woman _____<u>who wrote a popular novel</u>_____ came to our university

    last week.

2. The spaghetti is in a blue box. The spaghetti is on sale.

    The spaghetti _____ is on sale.

3. I usually go to the produce market. The produce market is on Van Avenue.

    I usually go to the produce market _____.

4. The man became president in 1993. The man was Bill Clinton.

    The man _____ was Bill Clinton.

5. I met the man. The man teaches chemistry at 9 o'clock.

    I met the man _____.

6. The students failed the test. The students need to take the test again.

    The students _____ need to take it again.

Now look at this sentence. Can you find the two clauses? Put parentheses around the extra clause. Can you find the two verbs and the two subjects in this sentence?

The man that we can see by the door works at the university.

The main verb is **works,** and the subject is **the man.** The second verb is **can see,** and the subject is **we.** Here the word **that** is not a subject. It is a connector. The analysis looks like this.

The <u>man</u> (that <u>we</u> <u>can see</u>) by the door <u>works</u> at the university.

Subject 1   Subject 2 Verb 2   Verb 1

Important: Notice the word **that** here is not the subject of a verb. In grammar, it is an object. In formal grammar, we do not use **who** here. We use **whom.** (If you need help with *who/whom,* see unit 7 in *Clear Grammar 1.*)

If a word is an object, it is not necessary. This means that you can omit the word **who/whom, that,** or **which** if you want, so for this usage, you have four possibilities.

SUMMARY: who/whom, that, which as object

People   *Things*

1. that   1. that
2. who (informal)   2. which
3. whom (formal)
4. Ø (nothing)   3. Ø (nothing)

1. The boy <u>that I saw</u> was tall.   1. The vase <u>that I took</u> was green.
2. The boy <u>who I saw</u> was tall.   2. The vase <u>which I took</u> was green.
3. The boy <u>whom I saw</u> was tall.   3. The vase <u>I took</u> was green.
4. The boy <u>I saw</u> was tall.

CAREFUL! Watch out for these common mistakes with relative pronouns as objects.

1. Do not use the wrong word to begin a relative clause. Do not use **which** for people or **who** for things in relative clauses.
   wrong: The man which we spoke to is Mr. O'Leary.
   correct: The man who we spoke to is Mr. O'Leary. (informal)
   correct: The man whom we spoke to is Mr. O'Leary. (formal)
   correct: The man that we spoke to is Mr. O'Leary.
   correct: The man we spoke to is Mr. O'Leary.

2. Do not include a pronoun after the verb of a relative clause.
   wrong: The man that we spoke to him is Mr. O'Leary.
   correct: The man that we spoke to is Mr. O'Leary.
   wrong: Jill sold her car to the woman who you know her.
   correct: Jill sold her car to the woman who you know. (informal)
   correct: Jill sold her car to the woman whom you know. (formal)

Exercise 5. Read the two sentences and then complete the new sentence. Follow the example.

1. The medicine is expensive. I took the medicine.

   The medicine _____ *that I took is expensive. (or : which, Ø)* _____ .

2. We didn't like the movie. Samantha recommended the movie.

   We didn't like the movie_____.

3. Do you have the CD? Ben bought the CD.

   Do you have the CD _____?

4. The weather report was wrong. Channel 7 gave a weather report.

   The weather report_____.

5. Did you taste the cake? Lynn made it.

   Did you taste the cake _____?

6. The newspaper was wet. We bought it.

   The newspaper _____.

Exercise 6. Read the sentence and then write a new sentence by including the second one within the first. Follow the example.

1. The young woman wrote a popular novel. The novel deals with crime in a rural town.

   The young woman wrote a popular novel that deals with crime in a rural town.

2. The young woman wrote a popular novel. All my friends have read the novel.

   _____

3. This is the letter. The letter was in a green envelope.

   _____

4. This is the letter. My cousin wrote the letter.

   _____

5. Did you buy the TV? The TV was on sale.

   _____

6. Did you buy the TV? You wanted the TV.

   _____

7. Do you understand the question? The question is at the top of the page.

   _____

8. Do you understand the question? You missed the question.

   _____

CHALLENGE   Can you combine these three sentences using relative clauses?

Have you seen the movie? The movie is about a president. The president was kidnapped

by terrorists. _____

Exercise 7.   Read the sentences. Draw a line under the relative clause. If the
               relative pronoun is optional, put parentheses around it. Follow the
               examples.

1. The student (that) the teacher called on is from Venezuela.

2. The student that arrived late is from Venezuela.

3. Do you ever watch the program that is on channel 8 at 3 P.M.?

4. What is the name of the cologne that you like so much?

5. I don't like the color of the dress that she bought.

6. The people who arrived even a little late couldn't get good seats.

7. I hate to eat fish that has a lot of bones.

8. The politician whom most people admire now in our state is a woman.

9. My friend said, "The woman who is speaking now is the CEO* at a huge corporation
   in Miami."

10. My friend said, "The woman who she is speaking to is the CEO at a huge corpora-
    tion in Miami."

11. I was reading a book that Becky gave me when I fell asleep.

12. Hank thinks that we should not buy products which contain leather.

*CEO = Chief Executive Officer

Exercise 8. Use the sentences to create a sentence with a relative clause that can complete these conversations. Omit all optional relative pronouns. Follow the example.

1. *Colin:* Did you bring an umbrella?

   Sadie: No. Why? The weather report for today didn't say rain.

   Colin: Well, _____the weather report I saw an hour ago said rain._____ .

   (The weather report said rain. I saw the weather report an hour ago.)

2. *Perry:* I wish I had some really good cookies.

   Matt: Well, _____.

   (Publix makes cookies. The cookies are not too sweet.)

   Perry: That sounds great, but Publix is closed at this time of night!

3. *Pam:* _____?

   (How was the test? You had the test yesterday.)

   Ian: I don't know. I thought it was easy, but I'll find out tomorrow.

4. *Jonah:* _____?

   (Did you like the rice dish? Lee cooked the rice dish.)

   Amy: It was pretty good. _____

   _____?

   (What do you call those vegetables? Those vegetables were in it.)

   Jonah: I'm not sure. Maybe they were some kind of pepper.

5. *Veronica:* _____?

   (Did you speak to the doctor? Mary spoke to the doctor.)

   Camilla: Actually, I think it was a different doctor. _____

   _____.

   (The doctor had red hair. I spoke to the doctor.)

CHALLENGE

"The person whom you should call is the director of customer complaints."

Do you think this sentence probably occurred in a conversation or in something written? Why?

Whose

I know the boy. The boy's mother works at the YMCA.
I know the boy whose mother works at the YMCA.

I know the boy. My cousin works with the boy's mother.
I know the boy whose mother my cousin works with.

When the two sentences talk about the same person, we can connect them with **who, that,** or **whom.** When the two sentences talk about the same thing, we can use **that** or **which.** However, when the second sentence has a possessive form of a word in the first sentence, then we can use **whose** to connect the two sentences.

example: The painter is Monet. I really like the painter's work the most.

whose

whose work I really like the most

The painter whose work I really like the most is Monet.

CAREFUL! Do not make these common mistakes.

1. Do not use **who's** for **whose.** They are completely different.
   wrong: The person who's car stopped at the corner is my neighbor.
   correct: The person whose car stopped at the corner is my neighbor.

2. Do not confuse **whose** for questions and **whose** for relative clauses. Both of these structures use the same word.
   correct: Whose keys are these?
   correct: I don't know whose keys you are holding.

Exercise 9.   Combine these sentences using *whose.* Follow the example.

1. I talked to the man. His son is in my art class.

   <u>   I talked to the man whose son is in my art class.   </u>

2. The students are listed on the first page. The students' last names begin with A.

   _____

3. The boy was so happy. His drawing won first prize in the contest.

   _____

4. We might play tennis with the woman. We know the woman's father.

   _____

5. We might play tennis with the woman. The woman's father won the club tournament.

   _____

6. Pilots will make less money. The pilots' contracts begin in January.

   _____

Optional Words: SUBJECT + *Be*

When a sentence has **who/which/that** as the subject and the verb is **be,** these two parts are optional. These words may be omitted without changing the meaning of the sentence. There are three main groups.

Prepositional phrases
   The magazines that are on the table are mine.
   The magazines on the table are mine.

Present participles
   People who are living in the dorm now will get a refund.
   People living in the dorm now will get a refund.

Past participles
   The students that were chosen for the contest were very happy.
   The students chosen for the contest were very happy.

CAREFUL! Watch out for these common mistakes.

1. Don't forget to omit both the subject and the verb **be.** You can't omit just one of them.
   wrong: The book that written in 1991 caused many problems.
   wrong: The book was written in 1991 caused many problems.
   correct: The book written in 1991 caused many problems.
   correct: The book that was written in 1991 caused many problems.

2. Don't omit any words if the verb **be** is not present.
   wrong: We called the people live next to us.
   correct: We called the people who live next to us.

Exercise 10.   Put parentheses around the words that are optional. Follow the example.

1. I talked to the man (who was) standing in front of the supermarket.

2. I asked the boys that were playing tennis what the time was.

3. Have you seen the movie that tells the story of the *Titanic's* maiden journey?

4. The Chinese restaurant that is near my house has great egg drop soup.

5. We chose three of the sandwiches which were on the table.

6. He was talking on the phone when someone knocked on the door.

7. I always mix up words that are spelled "ei" with words that are spelled "ie."

8. Plants that can stand hot, dry summers grow well in this area of the country.

9. Only two of the boys who wanted to work overtime were able to do it.

10. The child who is playing with the cat is my little sister.

Speaking Activity

Exercise 11.   Speaking Activity: Practice with Relative Clauses. What did you do yesterday?

Step 1.   Work with a partner. Student A should use the left column, and student B should use the right column. In each column, there are eight activities. Put a check mark (√) by any four of the activities.

Step 2. Do NOT show your book to your partner. Take turns asking each other questions. Use a relative clause and the word *yesterday* in every question. If the answer is YES, then you continue. If the answer is NO, then it is your partner's turn. Use relative clauses and the word *yesterday* in your questions and in your answers. Use complete sentences in your answers. You may use your partner's column to record which activities you have already asked about.

       examples: *A:* Did you see a bird that had bright blue feathers yesterday?
                  B: No, yesterday I didn't see a bird that had bright blue feathers. (The answer is NO, so it is B's turn.)
                  B: Did you talk to someone who was wearing a suit?
                  A: Yes, yesterday I talked to someone who was wearing a suit. (The answer is YES, so B asks again.)

The winner is the first student who can guess all four of his or her partner's answers.

Student A	*Student B*
____ use a pencil that had a sharp point	____ eat eggs that had ketchup on them
____ drink milk that didn't have any fat in it	____ see a bird that had bright blue feathers
____ talk to someone who was wearing a suit	____ use a pencil that didn't have an eraser
____ do all the homework Mr. Dell gave us	____ go to a store that was crowded
____ make a sandwich you couldn't eat	____ see a TV show you didn't like
____ see a cat that was black	____ drink tea which had lemon in it
____ eat toast that didn't have butter on it	____ call a friend who lives in another city
____ read the newspaper article that talked about tax laws	____ play tennis with the man who lives next to you

---

Speaking Activity

Exercise 12.   Speaking Practice. Have you ever seen a book that didn't have a cover?

Step 1. Make a list of five questions that practice *have you ever* and relative clauses.

examples: Have you ever flown on a plane that had engine problems
            during the flight?
            Have you ever seen a cat that didn't have a tail?
            Have you ever regretted buying something you bought
            because it was on sale?

Step 2. Work with a classmate (or interview a native speaker). If your partner
          answers YES, talk about that answer. Find out as much information as you
          can. For example, when did it happen? Where did it happen?

1. _____

2. _____

3. _____

4. _____

5. _____

**Speaking
Activity**

Exercise 13.   Speaking Activity. You are a detective who is trying to find out three
                 pieces of information about two people. You have the information
                 about one of the people. (Student A knows about the first person,
                 and student B knows about the second person.) Your goal is to find
                 out the information about the person that you do not know about.

Step 1. Work with a partner. One of you is student A, and one of you is student B.

Step 2. Put a check mark (√) by three pieces of information for the person you
          know about. Choose any three facts that you want.

Step 3. Take turns asking questions about the other person. If your partner's
          answer is YES, you may ask another question. If the answer is NO, then
          it's the other student's turn. Use one of these three clauses in your ques-
          tions.

                         the person who you know
                         the person whom you know
                         the person you know

example: Student A might ask: Does the person you know drive a red
                                 sports car?
            Student B might ask: Was the person that you know born
                                 in 1979?

Student A	Student B
___ have a gray cat	___ born in 1976
___ speak French	___ driven a red sports car since 1996
___ played tennis since 1985	___ have a white dog
___ from Morocco	___ travel to Chicago last week
___ work in Brazil in 1992	___ ever flown on the Concorde
___ born in 1979	___ speak English with a foreign accent
___ eat scrambled eggs for breakfast every day	___ always use a credit card to pay for things
___ go to Miami in 1997	___ sell computers for a living
___ gotten a phone call from someone in Russia	___ from Egypt

Exercise 14.   Multiple Choice. Circle the letter of the correct answer.

1. "How was the flight from Paris?"

   "I liked my seat, but Kathy didn't like _____."

   (A) the seat she got   (C) that she got

   (B) she got the seat   (D) the she got seat

2. Do you know the name of the director _____ movie we saw last week?

   (A) who   (C) whom

   (B) whose   (D) that was

3. Can you remember the name of the first book _____?

   (A) you read it   (C) you read

   (B) whose you read it   (D) whom you read

4. "Wow, look at all these CDs! Joe, are these yours?"

   "No, not all of the CDs _____ are mine."

   (A) are on the shelf   (C) that are on the shelf which

   (B) that are on the shelf   (D) that on the shelf

5. "What did you think about Greg's letter?"

   "Actually, I didn't have a chance to read _____."

   (A) the Greg wrote letter   (C) the letter wrote Greg

   (B) Greg wrote the letter   (D) the letter Greg wrote

6. In general, students _____ on campus this semester pay less for rent than

   students who are living off campus.

   (A) living   (C) whom are living

   (B) that living   (D) which live

7. "What beautiful handwriting! Who's that letter from?"

   "The person _____ was my best friend in college."

   (A) whose handwriting   (C) who wrote this letter

   (B) whom she wrote this letter   (D) writing this letter

8. "I would like to thank the numerous people _____ helped me when I was just

   starting my career. Without them, this award would not be possible."

   (A) whose   (C) whom

   (B) which   (D) that

Exercise 15.   Review Test

Part 1.   Read this short passage. Underline all relative
             clauses. Put parentheses ( ) around words that may
             be omitted.

   One of the most interesting countries that you can visit is

Venezuela. Venezuela is in the northern part of South America. The

countries which border on Venezuela are Brazil, Colombia, and

Guyana. Venezuela has four distinct geographical regions. The first

region is the Guiana Highlands. This area is an extensive area of

high plains and plateaus that extends from the Orinoco River to

the Brazilian border. Next, the area that lies between the Orinoco

River and the Andes Mountains is called the llanos. The llanos is a section of flat plains.

The third area of this country is the hot and humid coastal plain. This is the area which contains oil. It includes Lake Maracaibo and the Orinoco River delta. Finally, the region which is located in the southwestern corner of the country includes the high peaks of the Andes Mountains. Although all the people in Venezuela speak Spanish, the people who live in these four areas speak slightly differently from the people in the other areas. For example, the people who live in the Andes region of the country speak differently from other Venezuelans.

Part 2. Read this short passage. Fill in the missing words. Indicate all possible answers, including ∅ for places where nothing is also correct.

In December of last year, Meg Ripley wrote a book _____ has become a best seller. The name of the book was *Sitting at the Stop Sign*. This book is about a woman _____ was thinking about killing herself until an old friend unexpectedly came to see her. The friend didn't realize how bad the woman's life was, but by being there, the friend was able to make a few simple changes in the woman's life. The things _____ she did were not really very big, but they were big enough to affect the woman's outlook on life. I've never read a book _____ has affected me as much, either. If you read this book, perhaps there are things _____ you might learn about yourself, too. I highly recommend Ripley's story. A book _____ can touch the human heart and soul as much as this one can is definitely a book _____ everyone should read. My friends _____ I convinced to read this book continue to thank me for my recommendation.

Part 3. Read each sentence carefully. Look at the underlined part. If the underlined part is correct, circle the word *correct*. If it is wrong, circle the wrong part and write the correct form above.

correct   wrong   1. Pet <u>owners want</u> to walk their dogs in the park must use a leash.

correct   wrong   2. What's <u>the name of the car that you would like to buy</u>?

correct   wrong   3. Was your name on the envelope <u>which</u> I mailed for you?

correct   wrong   4. <u>Who's</u> the current prime minister of Canada?

correct   wrong   5. The answer <u>that I wrote it</u> on the test was incorrect.

correct   wrong   6. Can you remember the name of the <u>woman whom son</u> won the

race?

correct   wrong   7. Before you can get a refund, you have to fill out a form <u>that</u>

explains why you want to return the product.

Extra Writing Practice

Situation: You and three friends took a trip to a beach resort. You saw a brochure about the hotel that convinced you to stay there. The brochure promised "a view that would remain in your memory forever." It also mentioned "superb food that is prepared by skilled chefs" and "service that no other hotel could beat." The brochure also made numerous other promises. When you went to this resort, it was not good. The promises in the brochure were not true. Write a short letter of complaint to the manager of the hotel. Be sure to tell the manager exactly what was wrong.

Be sure to practice relative clauses from this unit. For example, you might say, "I expected to eat food <u>that was prepared by great chefs</u>, but the food <u>I ate</u> at your hotel was horrible." Always underline the grammar point that you have used so the teacher can see what you are trying to practice.

Answers to DISCOVER GRAMMAR on pages 116–17:

1. <u>The boy</u> (who is wearing a striped shirt) <u>is 12 years old</u>. main: The boy is 12 years old. extra: The boy is wearing a striped shirt. 2. <u>We came here on a jet</u> (that can carry over 400 people). main: We came here on a jet. extra: The jet can carry over 400 people. 3. <u>The man</u> (that has gray hair) <u>works with my father</u>. main: The man works with my father. extra: The man has gray hair. 4. <u>The owl</u> (that we saw at the zoo) <u>had huge eyes</u>. main: The owl had huge eyes. extra: We saw the owl at the zoo. 5. <u>We took a picture of the owl</u> (that we saw at the zoo). main: We took a picture of the owl. extra: We saw the owl at the zoo. 6. <u>The book</u> (which I bought) <u>was not very good</u>. main: The book was not very good. extra: I bought the book.   1. 1, people 2. 2, 3, 4, 5, both 3. 6, things

Unit 9

Infinitives and Gerunds

1. VERB + INFINITIVE
2. VERB + GERUND
3. VERB + INFINITIVE/GERUND
4. subject position
5. VERB + NOUN + INFINITIVE

What do you plan TO DO this weekend?

I would like TO GO to the beach, but my doctor told me to avoid GOING out in the sun during the middle of the day, so I don't know yet. What about you?

Discover Grammar

In six of these sentences, the underlined parts are wrong. Which underlined parts are wrong and which are correct? Put an X by the wrong sentences and a check mark (√) by the correct sentences.

_____ 1. The manager got angry because one of the employees kept on <u>talking</u> during the meeting.

_____ 2. Some people enjoy <u>going</u> to the beach, but I don't like it.

_____ 3. All of us are looking forward to <u>go</u> to the concert.

_____ 4. I hope <u>passing</u> the driver's license test tomorrow.

____ 5. Would you like <u>taking</u> a trip to San Francisco with me?

____ 6. The little girl pretended <u>being</u> sick, so her friend gave her some
          candy medicine.

____ 7. She promised <u>help</u> us with this work, but she didn't.

____ 8. Why did you decide <u>to enroll</u> in that computer course?

____ 9. When do you want <u>to buy</u> a new TV?

____10. I'm gaining weight! I have to avoid <u>eat</u> desserts and fried food.

Step 1. What do you think the grammar point is here? What is happen-
         ing? Why are some of the underlined parts correct and the others
         wrong? Write your ideas here.

         _____

         _____

         _____

         _____

Step 2. Work with a partner or in a small group. Discuss your answers.
         Can anyone explain what the grammatical structure (or rule) is
         here?

[Check p. 150 for the answers.]

Infinitives and Gerunds

You already know that you can use a noun after a verb. (These are called objects.) Here are
two examples.

1. I <u>want</u> <u>a sandwich</u>.   2. I <u>enjoyed</u> <u>the play</u>.

   VERB + NOUN/OBJECT   VERB + NOUN/OBJECT

Sometimes the idea that we want to express after the first verb is another verb. Look at the
same two examples.

3. I <u>want</u> **to eat** a sandwich.   4. I <u>enjoyed</u> **seeing** the play.

   VERB + **to** + **VERB**   VERB + **VERB** + **-ING**

        infinitive   gerund

In example 3, **to eat** is called an infinitive. An infinitive consists of **to** plus the simple verb.
In example 4, **seeing** is called a gerund. A gerund consists of a verb and **-ing.** (A gerund is
used as a noun.)

   In English, we use an infinitive after the verb **want.** (We cannot say, "I want eating.")
We use a gerund after **enjoy.** (We cannot say, "I enjoy to read.")

You have to remember which verbs use infinitives and which verbs use gerunds. There is nothing difficult to understand here. Some people prefer to memorize which verbs can use infinitives and which verbs can use gerunds. Other people prefer to practice example sentences again and again in order to get accustomed to which combinations sound correct. In order to learn this important information, you should use a method that works well for you.

Group 1. VERB + to + VERB	**Group 2. VERB + VERB + –ing**
(infinitive group)	(gerund group)
agree	avoid
decide	can't help
expect	consider
hope	enjoy
intend	finish
know how	get through★
learn	go (fishing, shopping, swimming)★★
need	insist on
offer	keep on
plan	look forward to
pretend	postpone
promise	put off
refuse	suggest
want	think about
would like	be tired of★★★
	be used to (See Unit 6.)

★See unit 2 for more examples of phrasal verbs.
★★A gerund is often used after **go** when the second verb refers to a sport or fun activity.
★★★See Units 6 and 7 for more examples of prepositions followed by gerunds.

CAREFUL! Do not make this common mistake.

Do not use infinitives after verbs that take gerunds (and vice versa).
wrong: Many parents avoid to give sweets to their kids.
correct: Many parents avoid giving sweets to their kids.

Exercise 1.   Underline the correct verb form. Follow the examples.

1. refuse   (doing, <u>to do</u>)   8. would like (doing, to do)   15. promise (doing, to do)

2. enjoy   (<u>doing</u>, to do)   9. be tired of (doing, to do)   16. learn   (doing, to do)

3. suggest (doing, to do)   10. know how (doing, to do)   17. agree   (doing, to do)

4. offer   (doing, to do)   11. insist on   (doing, to do)   18. avoid   (doing, to do)

5. decide   (doing, to do)   12. can't help   (doing, to do)   19. finish   (doing, to do)

6. expect   (doing, to do)   13. consider   (doing, to do)   20. intend   (doing, to do)

7. hope   (doing, to do)   14. postpone   (doing, to do)   21. pretend (doing, to do)

Exercise 2.   Write <u>to do</u> or <u>doing</u> on the lines. Follow the examples.

1. think about   ___*doing*___   6. put off   _____

2. need   ___*to do*___   7. know how   _____

3. be used to   _____   8. decide   _____

4. keep on   _____   9. get through _____

5. avoid   _____   10. would like _____

Exercise 3.   Underline the correct forms in these dialogues. Follow
                   the examples.

1. *Ellen:*   Would you like (going, <u>to go</u>) to the beach with us tomorrow?

   Ingrid: I don't know. I have a dentist's appointment tomorrow, but I might be able

              to put off (<u>going</u>, to go) to the dentist till the day after tomorrow since it's

              just a checkup. What time do you plan (leaving, to leave)?

   Ellen: We intend (leaving, to leave) at 7 A.M.

   Ingrid: 7 A.M.? Why do you want (leaving, to leave) that* early?

   Ellen: We thought about (going, to go) later, but we really want (avoiding, to

              avoid) (driving, to drive) in the morning rush hour. If we leave after 7,

              we'll get caught in traffic for sure.

   Ingrid: I don't know. Can I call you later? If I decide (going, to go) with you, I'll

              have to finish (doing, to do) some things around the house first.

   Ellen: Sure, Ingrid. Give me a call later.

---

*that + ADJECTIVE is the same as *so* + ADJECTIVE : *that early* means *so early*.

2. *Brian:* What's for dinner?

   Luke: Tuna fish sandwiches.

   Brian: Again? I'm really tired of (eating, to eat) tuna sandwiches.

   Luke: What? You don't like tuna fish? It's really healthy. Besides, I don't know how (cooking, to cook) anything else.

   Brian: OK, tuna may be healthy, but I can't eat it for dinner every night.

   Luke: Well, if you agree (eating, to eat) it just this one more time, I promise not (serving, to serve) it for dinner again.

   Brian: Ok. I just don't want (having, to have) (keeping on, to keep on) (eating, to eat) tuna for dinner!

3. *Zeke:* I just heard that you'll be on vacation next week.

   Paula: Yeah, that's right. I'm really looking forward to (taking, take) a few days off.

   Zeke: So what are you going to do?

   Paula: My husband wanted (going, to go) to St. Louis, but I wanted (going, to go) to New York.

   Zeke: So who won? Where have you decided (going, to go)?

   Paula: Well, last year my husband insisted on (going, to go) to Chicago even though I didn't want to. At first, I refused (going, to go) there. In the end, I agreed (going, to go) there but only after he promised (to let, letting) me choose this year's vacation spot.

   Zeke: So you're going to New York?

   Paula: Yes, we're leaving the day after tomorrow.

   Zeke: Do you plan (going, to go) (to sightsee, sightseeing) much there?

   Paula: Definitely. There are so many famous things to see there. I can't tell you how much both of us are looking forward to going there!

Speaking Activity

Exercise 4. Speaking Activity

Step 1. Work with a partner. Student A should look at both exercises 1 and 2. Student B should not look at the book at all.

Step 2. This is a timed activity. (Suggested time limit: two minutes) The teacher will say, "Ready, set, go!"

Step 3. Student A will call out verbs. Student B will say the verb plus any infinitive or gerund. If the answer is correct, student A will say, "That's correct" and then ask another verb. If the answer is wrong, student A will say, "No, that's not correct" and repeat the same verb. Student B must give the correct form but with a different word (i.e., he or she cannot use the same verb for the answer). The goal is for student B to get as many correct answers as possible in the time limit. When time is up, then students should reverse roles. The winner is the student who can get the most verbs correct in the time limit.

example: A: Need.
B: Need to go.
A: That's correct. Would like. (total: 1 point for B)
B: Would like reading.
A: No, that's not correct. Would like.
B: Would like to read.
A: No. The grammar is correct, but you have already used the verb *read*. You have to use a different word in the answer. Try again. Would like.
B: Would like to go. (total: 2 points for B)
A: That's correct. Know how. etc.

Group 3. Infinitive or Gerund = Same Meaning

Some verbs can be followed by either an infinitive or a gerund with no difference in meaning.

examples: If you <u>begin</u> **to cook** now, dinner will be ready by 7:30.
If you <u>begin</u> **cooking** now, dinner will be ready by 7:30.

VERB + to + VERB		**VERB + VERB + -ing**	
(infinitive group)		(gerund group)	
begin	continue	like	prefer
can't stand	hate	love	start

Exercise 5.   Write five original sentences with five of the verbs in this group:
begin, can't stand, continue, hate, like, love, prefer, start.

1. _____

2. _____

3. _____

4. _____

5. _____

Group 4. Infinitive or Gerund = Different Meanings

There are a few verbs that can be followed by either an infinitive or a gerund, but the meaning of the sentence is different. This group includes **remember, stop, try.**

remember

1. *Susan:* Here are the tomatoes that you asked me to buy.
   Sam: Thanks. I'm happy that you <u>remembered</u> **to buy** them.
   (First, she remembered them. Second, she bought them.)

2. *Chuck:* I found this old book with your name in it. Is it yours?
   Christy: Well, I don't <u>remember</u> **buying** it, but it must be mine if it has my
            name in it.
   (First, she bought it. Second, she didn't remember it.)

stop

1. *Allie:* Why are you late?
   Peter: My car was almost on empty, so I <u>stopped</u> **to get** some gas.
   ("**stop** + *to* + **VERB**" tells why. **To** is the same as **in order to**. See pp. 151–52.)

2. *Robert:* Does Stan still smoke?
   Cindy: No, he doesn't. He <u>stopped</u> **smoking** last May.
   ("**stop** + **VERB** + **-ing**" tells what he stopped.)

try★

1. *Anne:* Are you ready for today's test?
   Sally: I don't know. I <u>tried</u> **to learn** all the verbs, but it was difficult to do.
   ("**try** + **to** + **VERB**" = make an effort to do that action.)

2. *Phil:* Hey, this radio won't work.
   Jan: Why don't you <u>try</u> **turning** the switch to the right?
   ("**try** + **VERB** + **-ing**" = use another method or way to do something.)

★The difference between **try** + **INFINITIVE** and **try** + **GERUND** is not so great.

CAREFUL! Do not make this common mistake.

Do not change the meanings of certain verbs by using the wrong verb form.

wrong: We were tired, so we stopped to drive.

correct: We were tired, so we stopped driving.

Note: The first sentence is correct grammatically, but the meaning is different from the original idea.

Exercise 6. Underline the correct form. Be prepared to explain your choices. Follow the example.

1. We arrived at the party late because we had to stop (changing, <u>to change</u>) a flat tire.

2. If you can't fall asleep at night, try (counting, to count) sheep. It always works for me.

3. Hey, did you remember (getting, to get) some salt at the store?

4. It took me a long time to stop (smoking, to smoke), but I finally did it.

5. Wow. This picture is really old. It's in my box, but I don't remember (taking, to take) it.

6. I read in the paper that the stadium will stop (giving, to give) away tickets to any game.

7. The music was so good. It was hard to stop (dancing, to dance). We wanted to keep on, but it was getting late.

8. Look! There are a dozen eggs in this bag. I don't remember (buying, to buy) these eggs. They must be someone else's, and the store just made a mistake.

Gerund as Subject

Jack is in Dallas. He wants to go to Los Angeles to visit his cousin. He is trying to decide whether he should drive his car to Los Angeles or fly there. The distance is about 1,446 miles, but Jack has a new car that runs very well. What do you think he should do? Here are some of his thoughts.

Good Points for Driving
1. Driving might be good because he can see some interesting sights along the way.
2. Driving is fun. Driving gives him a lot of time to think about things.

Bad Points for Driving
1. Driving takes a long time.
2. Driving so many miles is more dangerous than flying.

Good Points for Flying
1. Flying is cheaper. (Round-trip airfare is only about $200 on some airlines.)
2. Flying is faster.

Bad Points for Flying
1. Flying to Los Angeles means that he will not have a car when he gets there.
2. Flying can be boring because you can't see anything except the sky.

When you want to use an action as the subject of a sentence, use a gerund. Remember that a gerund is a verb form that is actually used as a noun.

examples: <u>Driving</u> from Dallas to Los Angeles <u>takes</u> a long time.
subject   verb

CAREFUL! Do not make these common mistakes.

1. Do not use the wrong form as subject.
   wrong: Drive to Boston is more dangerous than fly there.
   uncommon:* To drive to Boston is more dangerous than to fly there.
   correct: Driving to Boston is more dangerous than flying there.

2. Don't use a plural verb form with a gerund. Don't be tricked by the object after the gerund. The object of a gerund does not affect the verb.
   wrong: Eating green vegetables are good for your health.
   correct: Eating green vegetables is good for your health.
   (**Eating** is the subject. **Vegetables** is not the subject. You need a singular verb, so you use **is**.)
   wrong: Choosing a car and maintaining it is two different things.
   correct: Choosing a car and maintaining it are two different things.
   (**Choosing** and **maintaining** together are the subject. You need a plural verb, so you use **are**.)

*It is possible to use an infinitive in the subject position sometimes. However, in conversation and informal writing, an infinitive is almost never used. In general, avoid using infinitives as subjects until you have seen more examples in literary or formal contexts. If you see or hear a sentence that begins with **to** + **VERB**, it is probably not being used as the subject but rather as an adverbial phrase telling why: <u>To pass that course</u>, you have to study really hard and do all the homework. (See pp. 151–52 for more information on this construction.)

VERB + NOUN/PRONOUN + to + VERB

1. **I want** <u>to go</u> to the post office.
2. **I want** Mike <u>to go</u> to the post office.

What is the difference between these two sentences? Both are correct, but the meanings are different.

Both sentences have the verb **want** and an infinitive. In the first sentence, there is one subject (**I**) and two verbs (**want** and **to go**). This means that "I want" and "I go." In other words, one person is doing both actions.

In the second sentence, there are two subjects (**I** and **Mike**) and two verbs (**want** and **to go**). In this sentence, one person is doing the first action ("I want"), and another person is doing the second action ("Mike goes").

Now read these situations and the sentence that describes each situation.

1. *Situation:*   The teacher said, "Do the exercise on page 19."
   Description: The teacher told the students to do the exercise on page 19.
2. *Situation:*   "Jean, please call Ahmed as soon as possible."
   Description: I want Jean to call Ahmed as soon as possible.

The new sentences have two verbs. The first verb is a verb that asks or tells someone to do something. The second verb is the action.

> *example 1:* The teacher <u>told</u> us <u>to do</u> the exercise on page 19.
>   Verb 1 Verb 2
>
> *example 2:* I <u>want</u> Jean <u>to call</u> Ahmed as soon as possible.
>   Verb 1   Verb 2

Notice that the first verbs are often similar in meaning. These verbs often ask or tell someone to do something.

advise	invite	tell
allow	need	urge
ask	order	want
expect	permit	would like
force	persuade	
get	teach	

The basic pattern here is the following.

Someone	+	VERB	+	Someone	+ to	+	VERB.	
I		would like		you	to		help	me tonight.
She		asked		Kevin	to		lend	her some money.
The president		told		the soldiers	to		do	their best.
The boss would		like		us	to		attend	next week's meeting.

Special Problem: *Say* **and** *Tell*

English has two different verbs: **say** and **tell.** Some languages have only one verb for these two English verbs. **Say** and **tell** use different grammatical structures.

> *example 1:* The speaker is talking to or about another person.
> > **person + say, + "** **[exact words]** **"** He said, "Leave!"
> > **person + tell + person + INFINITIVE** He told the students to leave.
> *example 2:* The speaker is talking about himself.
> > **person + say, + "** **[exact words]** **"** He said, "I'm hungry."
> > **person + tell + [sentence]★** He said he was★ hungry.

★This is called reported or indirect speech. The verb in direct speech is in the tense that the person actually used when he or she spoke. The tense of the verb in reported speech depends on the situation.

CAREFUL! Do not make these common mistakes.

1. Do not use a structure from your language for this grammar. (Never use **that + subject + VERB** with these verbs.)
   wrong: I want that you eat dinner with me tonight.
   correct: I want you to eat dinner with me tonight.
   wrong: The supervisor ordered that the workers come in at 8:30.
   correct: The supervisor ordered the workers to come in at 8:30.

2. Do not forget to use an infinitive. Do not use a simple form of the verb or a gerund.
   wrong: Would you ask Maggie lend us some money?
   wrong: Would you ask Maggie lending us some money?
   correct: Would you ask Maggie to lend us some money?

3. Do not add **–s, –ed, –ing,** or any other endings on the second verb. The first verb can change (according to singular/plural or tense), but the second verb does not change.
   wrong: He wants Carol to goes with us.
   correct: He wants Carol to go with us.
   (Only the first verb can have **–s** for **he, she, it.**)
   wrong: In 1974, the government ordered people to stopped using leaded fuel.
   correct: In 1974, the government ordered people to stop using leaded fuel.
   (Only the first verb can be in past tense because of 1974.)

4. Do not confuse **say** and **tell.** They use different grammatical structures.
   wrong: He said me to call the hospital.
   correct: He told me to call the hospital.

Exercise 7.   Editing. If the underlined part is correct, write C on the line. If the underlined part is wrong, write the correction (substitution) on the line.

_____C_____   1. The director <u>needs everyone to help</u> on this project.

____made them do____   2. The parents <u>made them to do</u> their homework.

_____   3. Would you please <u>ask him call</u> us later?

_____   4. My doctor <u>advised me to start</u> exercising more.

_____   5. How long do you <u>expect us to wait</u>?

_____   6. I don't know how she <u>got everyone agree</u> on the plan.

_____   7. Parents <u>would like their kids eat</u> all their vegetables.

_____   8. Will the airline <u>allow me change</u> my flight now?

_____   9. The general <u>ordered the soldiers to shoot</u> at the enemy.

_____   10. Zack refuses to go. Perhaps LeAnn can <u>persuade him go</u>.

_____   11. Who <u>told you do</u> this?

_____   12. The politician said, "I <u>urge you to vote</u> for me today!"

FOR MORE ADVANCED STUDENTS: make, let, have; help

There are four other verbs that are similar to this last group. These verbs are usually followed by a person and another verb. However, the verb that comes after the object with these four verbs follows a different pattern.

make, let, have: The second verb is the simple base form of the verb. Study the examples.

    make: She made the children <u>eat</u> their vegetables.

    let: She let the children <u>play</u> outside.

    have: She had* the children <u>do</u> their homework first.

help: The second verb can be simple base form or an infinitive. Both are equally correct.

    help: Can you help me <u>carry</u> these boxes to the basement?

    help: Can you help me <u>to carry</u> these boxes to the basement?

*"have someone do something" means that someone else does the work for you because you paid that person, because you are in a power position (mother-child), or because you asked him or her.

Exercise 8.   Write two examples for each verb. Try to write about real examples.

1. make _____

2. make _____

3. let _____

4. let _____

5. have _____

6. have _____

7. help _____

8. help _____

Exercise 9.   Multiple Choice. Circle the letter of the correct answer.

1. "Did the students talk to the guidance counselor?"

    "Yes, she _____ them find a tutor."

    (A) suggested   (C) wanted

    (B) helped   (D) looked forward to

2. "Are you _____ to France again next month?"

   "Actually, I'd love to go there again."

   (A) considering to go   (C) letting to go

   (B) considering going   (D) letting going

3. "Do you have any problems when you fly on long trips?"

   "No, never. _____ is the best way to travel."

   (A) To fly   (C) Flying

   (B) To flying   (D) Fly

4. "How did you and your family go to India?"

   "My dad wanted us to go by ship, but the rest of us simply refused _____ that."

   (A) doing   (C) done

   (B) do   (D) to do

5. "So what did you do when the microwave caught fire?"

   "Well, of course I stopped _____ TV and ran to the kitchen."

   (A) to watch   (C) watch

   (B) watching   (D) watched

6. "My car is giving me problems. I don't know what's wrong."

   "Why don't you have the people at Frank's Garage _____ a look at it? They're very

      good with all kinds of cars."

   (A) taken   (C) taking

   (B) to take   (D) take

7. "If you didn't want to go to the mall, then why did you go?"

   "Vance _____ going."

   (A) made us   (C) promised

   (B) insisted on   (D) wanted

8. "Did you see what happened when she read the letter?"

   "Yes, I did. As soon as she opened the envelope, she started _____."

   (A) cry   (C) crying

   (B) the cry   (D) to crying

Exercise 10.   Review Test

Part 1.   Read this short conversation. Fill in the blanks with the correct form of the verb given.

Dean: I'm thinking of _____ (go) to the soccer match tomorrow afternoon. Is

anyone interested in _____ (go) with me?

Joy: I'd certainly like _____ (see) that match! Brad, how about you? Do you

want _____ (go)?

Brad: Well, _____ (go) to that match would be great, but I have to get

through _____ (write) this book report for English class before I can

consider _____ (go) anywhere!

Dean: Haven't you finished _____ (write) that paper yet?

Joy: Brad, what are you doing? You can't use a pencil to write that paper.

Brad: What do you mean?

Joy: The teacher told us _____ (use) a word processor for the paper. I never

heard the teacher say this, so I wrote mine in pencil, too.

Brad: And?

Joy: He refused _____ (accept) it. He had me _____ (do) it again.

Brad: OK, that settles it. I don't want _____ (write) this paper again, but it

looks like I don't have a choice. Sorry, guys, but I can't go to the game. I need

_____ (stop) _____ (write) this paper in pencil and start

_____ (do) it on a word processor.

Part 2.   Read each sentence carefully. Look at the underlined part. If the underlined part is correct, circle the word *correct.* If it is wrong, circle the wrong
part and write the correct form above.

correct   wrong   1. He <u>told us to wait</u> for him at the corner of Green and Wilcox.

correct   wrong   2. <u>To drive there take</u> eight hours.

correct   wrong   3. If you want flowers in the garden in May, you <u>have to plant</u> the

seeds by March.

correct   wrong   4. In what year did the government <u>stop allowing</u> the advertising of

tobacco on TV?

correct   wrong   5. If you don't <u>learn to swim</u> as a child,

correct   wrong   you might never <u>know to swim</u>.

Extra Writing Practice

Situation: Write a dialogue between three friends who are trying to decide what to do next Saturday. Try to let each of the three friends speak four or five times.

Be sure to practice the gerunds and infinitives from this unit. For example, one person might say, "What do you guys <u>want to do</u> this weekend?" or "Oh, no. You guys aren't going to <u>force me to go</u> to the zoo again. I didn't <u>enjoy going</u> there last time, so I don't want to go again!" Always underline the grammar point that you have used so the teacher can see what you are trying to practice.

Answers to DISCOVER GRAMMAR, pages 135–36:

1. √ 2. √ 3. X 4. X 5. X 6. X 7. X 8. √ 9. √ 10. X The form of the underlined verb depends on the verb that comes before it. Some verbs must be followed by an infinitive (*to* + VERB), while others must be followed by a gerund (VERB + -*ing*). It is necessary to remember which verbs require infinitives and which require gerunds.

Unit 10

Connectors

1. *in order to* vs. *to* vs. *for*
2. *and . . . too/so/either/neither*
3. *however, therefore, so*

Venezuela is in South America, AND SO is Ecuador.
Venezuela exports oil, AND Ecuador does, TOO.

Connecting a Purpose with the Stem of a Sentence

example 1: A: Why did you come to this school in England?
B: I came here <u>to</u> learn English.

example 2: A: Why do you leave your house so early in the morning?
B: I leave early <u>in order to</u> avoid the rush-hour traffic.

example 3: A: Why did you go to the store?
B: I went to the store <u>for</u> some bread.

All three of these patterns express the same meaning. The grammatical difference is what comes after the connecting word.

to **+ VERB**	in order to **+ VERB**	for **+ NOUN**

> *examples:* I went to the post office <u>to buy</u> some stamps.
>
> I went to the post office <u>in order to buy</u> some stamps.
>
> I went to the post office <u>for</u> some stamps.

CAREFUL! Do not make these common mistakes.

1. Do not use **for** with a verb. (This is a very common mistake!)
   wrong: I came here for learn English.
   correct: I came here to learn English.

2. Do not use **to** with a noun when you should use **for.**
   wrong: I'm going to the store <u>to</u> bread.
   correct: I'm going to the store <u>for</u> bread.

Exercise 1.   Questions with *why* often have three possible answers. Make questions with *why* and give three possible answers. Follow the example.

example: The customer called the waiter to ask for more water.

    <u>Why did the customer call the waiter</u>   ?

    <u>To ask for more water</u>   .

    <u>In order to ask for more water</u>   .

    <u>For more water</u>   .

1. She drove to the mall to pick up her children's photos.

    _____?

    _____.

    _____.

    _____.

2. Some kids are collecting money to help the storm victims.

    _____?

    _____.

    _____.

    _____.

3. To get fresh bread, Mrs. McDowell usually goes to that deli.

_____?

_____.

_____.

_____.

───────

Exercise 2.   Write *to* or *for* on the line in order to answer the question *why.*
Follow the examples.

> *examples:* He came here ____*to*____ learn English.
> He came here ____*for*____ better English skills.

1. I'm going to the department store _____ a new tie. Do you want to go there

   _____ help me choose one?

2. When you called, I was studying _____ my math test tomorrow. Hey, can I

   borrow your calculator? I'd like to use it _____ do the problems on the test.

3. You can call me _____ ask any questions you want. Maybe I can help you

   _____ understand this lesson.

4. Josephine opened the drawer _____ get a spoon. She only found small ones, so

   she opened a few more drawers _____ a larger one.

5. I just saw a great job listed in the newspaper, but I need to speak French and Spanish

   fluently _____ this position. _____ learn to speak Spanish and French, I'm

   considering enrolling in an intensive language course. What do you think of this idea?

Repeating an Idea in the Second Part of a Sentence

Sometimes a sentence consists of one part that states new information about "A" and a second part that says, "B, too" or "the same thing is true about B." For example, if one sentence is "Nancy plays tennis well" and the second sentence is "Milton plays tennis well," what is the usual way to express these two ideas in one sentence in English?

In this case, it is not good to say all the words of both parts. Thus, it is not good to say, "Nancy plays tennis well and Milton plays tennis well." This does not sound good, although it is grammatically correct.

In this case, it is not necessary to repeat all of the words in the second part. We usually cut the information in the second part in a special way. In English there are four ways to express the idea of "B, too."

1. Nancy plays tennis well, and Milton does too.
2. Nancy plays tennis well, and so does Milton.
3. Nancy doesn't play basketball well, and Milton doesn't either.
4. Nancy doesn't play basketball well, and neither does Milton.

1 and 2 have the same meaning. Both parts are affirmative.
3 and 4 have the same meaning. Both parts are negative.

If the sentences have a verb, then do not repeat the verb in the second part. Use an auxiliary verb such as **do, does,** or **did** (depending on the subject of the sentence and the tense of the verb).

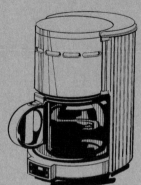

> *example:*   José likes coffee. Rita <u>likes</u> coffee.
>   José likes coffee, and Rita <u>does</u> too.

If the sentences have the verb **be** or a modal, then use a form of **be** or the modal in the second part.

> *example:*   I am tired. She is tired.
>   I am tired, and she is too.

Notice that the word order after **so** and **neither** is inverted.

> *examples:*   I like tea, <u>and she does too</u>.   vs.
>   I like tea, <u>and so does she</u>.
>
>   Beth might not go to the concert, <u>and I might not either</u>. vs.
>   Beth might not go to the concert, <u>and neither might I</u>.

Notice that **neither** is already negative. Do not use **neither** and **not** together.

Remember: When there are two affirmative sentences, use **and . . . too** OR **and so . . .**
When there are two negative sentences, use **and . . . either** OR **and neither . . .**

CAREFUL! Do not make these common mistakes.

1. Do not repeat the whole sentence in the second part.
   wrong: I arrived to class late, and Raymond arrived to class late.
   correct: I arrived to class late, and Raymond did too.

2. Don't repeat the (whole) verb in the second part. Use an auxiliary verb (**do, does, did;** modals; **am, is, are** for present progressive; **was, were** for past progressive; **have, has** for present perfect).
   wrong: Frank speaks German, and Patty speaks too.
   correct: Frank speaks German, and Patty does too.

wrong: She was watching TV, and I was watching TV too.
correct: She was watching TV, and I was too.

wrong: Irene has lived here for five years, and I have lived here for five years, too.
correct: Irene has lived here for five years, and I have too.

3. Don't use the wrong word in the second part. Pay attention to the verb that is used in the first sentence.
    wrong: Victor made 100 on the test, and I am too.
    correct: Victor made 100 on the test, and I did too.

    wrong: Barbara knows how to drive well, and so am I.
    correct: Barbara knows how to drive well, and so do I.

4. Don't repeat **have** when it is a main verb. All verbs in English use an auxiliary in the second part.
    wrong: Jeremy has a red car, and I have too.
    correct: Jeremy has a red car, and I do too.

5. Don't forget to invert the word order with **so** and **neither.**
    wrong: I speak French fluently, and so Dan does.
    correct: I speak French fluently, and so does Dan.

    wrong: Kelly doesn't like winter weather, and neither Mary does.
    correct: Kelly doesn't like winter weather, and neither does Mary.

6. Don't use two negatives with **neither.**
    wrong: Linda hasn't eaten lunch yet, and neither hasn't Kareen.
    correct: Linda hasn't eaten lunch yet, and neither has Kareen.

    wrong: April doesn't have thirty-one days, and neither doesn't June.
    correct: April doesn't have thirty-one days, and neither does June.

7. Don't use **so, too, either,** or **neither** if one sentence is affirmative and one is negative. In this "mixed" case, use **but.** (I like vanilla ice cream. Jenny doesn't like vanilla ice cream.)
    wrong: I like vanilla ice cream, and Jenny doesn't either.
    correct: I like vanilla ice cream, but Jenny doesn't.

Exercise 3.   Affirmative Sentences. Write the second part of the sentence. Write both possible answers. Follow the examples.

1. Keith learned to play tennis when he was a kid. Ken learned to play tennis when he was a kid.

    Keith learned to play tennis when he was a kid,____and Ken did too____.

    Keith learned to play tennis when he was a kid,____and so did Ken____.

2. Tony is going to buy a new house. His cousin is going to buy a new house.

    Tony is going to buy a new house, _____.

    Tony is going to buy a new house, _____.

3. The United States has a long coastline. Chile has a long coastline.

    The United States has a long coastline,_____.

    The United States has a long coastline,_____.

4. This plane can hold 260 passengers. That plane can hold 260 passengers.

    This plane can hold 260 passengers, _____.

    This plane can hold 260 passengers, _____.

5. Vanessa hates onions in her food. Wanda hates onions in her food.

    Vanessa hates onions in her food, _____.

    Vanessa hates onions in her food, _____.

6. I have to learn English to enter this college. Bo has to learn English to enter this college.

    I have to learn English to enter this college, _____.

    I have to learn English to enter this college, _____.

CHALLENGE   One student says that the answer to number 6 is "and Bo has too." A second student says that the answer is "and Bo does too." Who is correct?   More importantly, why did you choose the answer that you did?

Exercise 4. Negative Sentences. Write the second part of the sentence. Write both possible answers. Follow the examples.

1. Cary doesn't do any sports. Ted doesn't do any sports.

    Cary doesn't do any sports, __and Ted doesn't either_____.

    Cary doesn't do any sports, __and neither does Ted_____.

2. Nathan shouldn't smoke so much. You shouldn't smoke so much.

    Nathan shouldn't smoke so much, _____.

    Nathan shouldn't smoke so much, _____.

3. We didn't eat out last night. The Sawyers didn't eat out last night.

    We didn't eat out last night, _____.

    We didn't eat out last night, _____.

4. English class isn't that hard. Science class isn't that hard.

    English class isn't that hard,

    _____.

    English class isn't that hard,

    _____.

5. Alison didn't take her car to work today. I didn't take my car to work today.

    Alison didn't take her car to work today,

    _____.

    Alison didn't take her car to work today,

    _____.

6. George doesn't have a new stereo. I don't have a new stereo.

    George doesn't have a new stereo, _____.

    George doesn't have a new stereo, _____.

Exercise 5. Write *and* or *but* on the lines. Follow the example.

1. She hates bell peppers, ___but___ I don't.

2. Ice cream is fattening, _____ yogurt isn't.

3. January has thirty-one days, _____ so does August.

4. Benny has gone to Europe several times, _____ I haven't.

5. Last month's electricity bill was really high, _____ so was this month's.

6. I ordered a cheese pizza at the restaurant, _____ Janette and Lim did too.

7. Kuwait has a very hot climate, _____ England doesn't.

8. Kuwait has a very hot climate, _____ Egypt does too.

9. Kuwait has a very hot climate, _____ so does Saudi Arabia.

10. This machine doesn't give change, _____ that one doesn't either.

Exercise 6.   Read the sentences and then complete them with the missing words. Follow the examples.

1. I need a new dictionary, and I think you _____ *do too* _____.

2. They didn't understand the lesson, and _____ *neither did* _____ I.

3. Red is too bright for a pair of pants, and yellow _____.

4. Red is too bright for a pair of pants, and _____ yellow.

5. Red is too bright for a pair of pants, but dark blue _____.

6. Peter couldn't wake up on time today, and I _____.

7. Tim has brown hair and green eyes, and his sister _____.

8. Tim doesn't have curly hair, and _____ his sister.

9. Tim doesn't have curly hair, but his sister _____.

10. Tim doesn't have curly hair, and his sister _____.

11. I have a dark blue umbrella, and _____ Sherry.

12. I have had a blue umbrella for over a year, and Sherry _____.

13. Mexicans speak Spanish, and _____ Colombians.

14. Some Korean food is spicy, and some Mexican food _____.

15. Some Korean food is spicy, but British food _____.

Speaking Activity

Exercise 7.   Speaking Activity

This chart gives information about four people and eight actions or situations. The words *yes* or *no* in the chart refer to that person and that action. For example, *yes* under Tomoko's name by "likes iced tea" means that Tomoko likes iced tea. The *no* under Sani's name in the same line means that Sani doesn't like tea.

Step 1.   Look at the chart below. On page 160, write ten statements about the people and the information. Make some of the statements true and some false. Practice *and . . . too, and so . . . , and . . . either, and neither . . . ,* and *but.* Circle T for true or F for false to indicate whether your sentence is really true or false.

Step 2.   Work with a partner. Student A will read all of his or her sentences. Student B will look at the book and say true or false for each statement. Keep track of the number of correct answers.

Step 3.   After partner A has read all of his or her sentences, then it is student B's turn and student A must say true or false for each statement.

Action/Situation	Tomoko (female)	Thomas (male)	Sani (male)	Amina (female)
likes iced tea	yes	yes	no	no
has gone to Mexico before	no	yes	yes	no
speaks Spanish fluently	no	yes	no	no
bought a car last year	yes	no	no	yes
has a bike	no	yes	yes	yes
is a quiet person	no	no	yes	yes
can play the piano	no	yes	yes	no
might move soon	yes	yes	no	yes

T F 1. _____

T F 2. _____

T F 3. _____

T F 4. _____

T F 5. _____

T F 6. _____

T F 7. _____

T F 8. _____

T F 9. _____

T F 10. _____

Speaking Activity

Exercise 8.　　Speaking Activity

Work in groups of three students. Students will take turns speaking for one minute. One student will speak, one student will be the timekeeper, and the other student will be the "grammar judge." All students should look at the chart in the previous exercise. One student will say, "Ready, set, go!" and then the speaker should begin with any true sentence about the chart. All sentences must practice *and . . . too, and so . . . , and . . . either, and neither . . . ,* or *but.* Each correct sentence that is completed within the one-minute time limit gets one point. If the speaker is in the middle of a sentence when the timekeeper says, "Time," the speaker does not receive any points for that sentence.

However, Therefore, So

1. **However** is used to connect two sentences. **However** is similar in meaning to **but.** It is used to contrast two different ideas.

   But is a conjunction and can only occur (in formal writing) in the middle of a single sentence. **However** can occur in one sentence or it can start the second sentence. In the first case, it is preceded by a semicolon (;) and followed by a comma (,). In the second case, one sentence should have a period at the end, the **h** in **however** should be capitalized because it is now the first word of a sentence, and there should be a comma (,) after **however.**

   The teacher reviewed the material for three days; however, six students failed the exam.
   The teacher reviewed the material for three days. However, six students failed the exam.

2. **Therefore** is used when the second sentence is a logical idea based on the first sentence. It is similar in meaning to the word **so.**

    Therefore can occur in one sentence or it can start the second sentence. In the first case, it is preceded by a semicolon (;) and followed by a comma (,). In the second case, one sentence should have a period at the end, the **t** in **therefore** should be capitalized because it is now the first word of a sentence, and there should be a comma (,) after **therefore.**

> The students wanted to do well on the final exam; therefore, everyone studied very hard.
> The students wanted to do well on the final exam. Therefore, everyone studied very hard.

3. **So** has two meanings. One of them means a result; the other means a purpose.

    Sometimes **so** means a result. It means that the second sentence is a result of the information in the first sentence. In this case, **so** cannot begin the sentence. It only occurs in the middle of the written sentence and should have a comma before it.

> Jackie studied her notes carefully, so no one was surprised when she gave a great speech.
> My printer ran out of ink, so I had to go to the office supply store this morning.

    Sometimes **so** means purpose or reason for doing something. It means that the second sentence tells or explains why the information in the first sentence happened. In this case, **so** cannot begin the sentence. It only occurs in the middle of the written sentence. Note that it does NOT have a comma before it. In spoken English, there is no pause or break before the second part of the sentence. It is common to use **can, could, will,** or **would** in the second clause.

> I bought ten soft drinks so I would have enough drinks for everyone at my party.
> Please arrive early so you'll be able to get a good parking place.

Exercise 9.   Fill in the blanks with the words *however, therefore,* or *so.* Use the sentence meaning and punctuation to help you figure out the right answers. Follow the example.

1. *Max:*   I'm going to the pet store _____so_____ I can buy some more cat food. Do you want to go?

   Melinda: Well, I have a lot of work to do. _____, I think I ought to get out of the house for a while, _____ I'll go with you.

2. *Caroline:* Why did you call up Terry?

   Larry: I called him up _____ I'd know what time I have to work tomorrow.

   He has a copy of the complete schedule.

3. *Heidi:* This book is missing some of the pages, _____ I'm going

   to return it.

   Ron: Can you do that? I thought they didn't take any returns.

   Heidi: You can't return a book because you don't like it. _____, you can

   return a book if the book itself is defective. This one is defective.

   _____, they will accept it without any problem.

4. *Kirk:* What did you think of that movie? I heard it wasn't that good,

   _____ I decided not to go see it.

   Sheila: Several movie critics gave negative reports on the movie; _____, I

   decided to go see it anyway.

Exercise 10. Punctuation. Add punctuation if it is needed. You may also need to add capital letters. Follow the example.

1. The little boy wanted to buy a gift for his mother **;** however **,** he didn't have enough
   money. (OR mother **.** However **,**)

2. Health care in the U.S. is very expensive so many people don't have any health
   insurance.

3. Health care in the U.S. is not free however in Canada the situation is very different.

4. Vietnam was a French colony for many years therefore French is spoken in some
   parts.

5. The price of tickets for the concert is $50 however the tickets are selling very quickly.

6. The flight was overbooked therefore some passengers were denied boarding.

7. Yvonne cooked a huge pot of stew so everyone would be able to eat some at the
   party.

8. Yvonne cooked a huge pot of stew so everyone was able to eat some at the party.

Speaking Activity

Exercise 11a.   Speaking Activity: Crossword Puzzle, Student A

Two students work together. Use the clues on this page to fill in as many of the words as possible. Then take turns asking each other questions about the information that is missing from the puzzle. Student A works on the first crossword puzzle while student B works on the second crossword puzzle. Do NOT look at your partner's puzzle at any time.

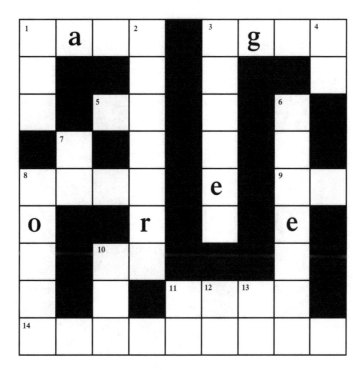

Across

1. Debby went to the post office to _____ a letter.
5. I arrived _____ noon, but he didn't.
9. you and I
11. You need a helmet to _____ a bicycle here.

Down

1. March has 31 days, and so does _____.
3. Blair doesn't like broccoli, and his son doesn't _____.
6. He has a nice car. _____, he prefers to walk to work if the weather's good.
8. one book, two books, three books, etc.
11. a prefix that means again

Speaking Activity

Exercise 11b.   Speaking Activity: Crossword Puzzle, Student B

Two students work together. Use the clues on this page to fill in as many of the words as possible. Then take turns asking each other questions about the information that is missing from the puzzle. Student B works on the second crossword puzzle while student A works on the first crossword puzzle. Do NOT look at your partner's puzzle at any time.

	1		i	2		3			4
			e						
	5						6		
7			h						
8						9			
u	10						v		
		11	12	13					
14		r							

Across

3. He wanted to make an omelette, so he went to the store for some _____.
8. You have to wake up earlier in order to _____ to class on time.
10. Madrid is in Spain, and so _____ Barcelona.
14. A score over 80 is passing. Heather made 83. _____, she passed the exam.

Down

2. He got some stamps to mail some _____.
4. Pedro's from Mexico, and _____ is Ana.
7. In order to _____ the dishes well, you need some dish detergent.
10. frozen water
12. _____ you want to rent a car, you need a valid driver's license.
13. He speaks French, and I _____ too.

Exercise 12.   Multiple Choice. Circle the letter of the correct answer.

1. *Melissa:* "What did you two do yesterday?"

    Diane: "I went to the library, and _____ Maria."

    (A) went too   (C) did too

    (B) so went   (D) so did

2. She didn't have her key, but Karen _____.

    (A) had   (C) did

    (B) has   (D) didn't

3. We ate pie for dessert, and they _____ .

    (A) did too   (C) did either

    (B) ate too   (D) neither did

4. He is attending that school specifically _____ get computer training.

    (A) for   (C) in order

    (B) so   (D) to

5. _____, and so does Martha.

    (A) I never eat out   (C) I don't do well in English class

    (B) I have gone to France   (D) I have a white car

6. *Tom:* "Did you understand the word?"

    Steve: "Yes, I did, and so _____ the other students."

    (A) did   (C) understood

    (B) were   (D) had

7. The Wilton charges $90 a night, _____ we decided to look for a cheaper hotel.

    (A) therefore   (C) for

    (B) so   (D) in order to

8. "Can you go with me to the furniture store tomorrow? I'd like to hear your input."

    "Sure. I can go in the morning, and I think Paula _____."

    (A) goes too   (C) so goes

    (B) can too   (D) so can

Exercise 13.   Review Test

Part 1.   Underline the correct answers.

1. *Nadine:*   Did Anna go to Knoxville (therefore, for, to) get information about a

    university there?

    Robert: Yes, she went there two days ago, and (so did, so went, so was) Patricia.

2. *Kathy:*   Each question was worth four points. I missed three questions.

    (So, Therefore, Neither), my score should be 88, not 78.

    Teacher: Kathy, your math is correct. (However, But, In order to), you also forgot to

    answer the final essay question, and that was worth ten points, (therefore, so,

    for) that's why your score really is 78.

3. Using prefixes and suffixes in English can be useful; (therefore, however, so), some-

    times they cause problems. For example, the prefix "pre-" in English usually means

    "before" as in "precede" or "previous." (Therefore, However, So), sometimes the three

    letters "pre" are not really a prefix with the same meaning. Examples of this are

    "pretty" and "prefer." Students of English as a second or foreign language should

    study words carefully (for, so, in order to) be able to understand the meaning of a new

    word well.

Part 2.   Read each sentence carefully. Look at the underlined part. If the underlined part is correct, circle the word *correct*. If it is wrong, circle the wrong
part and write the correct form above.

correct   wrong   1. I called Joe to see how he was feeling, and Mark <u>did too</u>.

correct   wrong   2. Doughnuts are very fattening, <u>and</u> cake isn't.

correct   wrong   3. That automobile is very expensive.<u> However,</u> many people are

    buying it because it really is such a good car.

correct   wrong   4. I really want to go to Hawaii, and my wife <u>doesn't either</u>.

correct   wrong   5. May has thirty-one days, but September <u>hasn't</u>.

correct   wrong   6. Madonna stopped making records for a while <u>for</u> take care of her

    new child.

correct   wrong   7. This computer cost less than $1,000, and that one <u>does too</u>.

correct   wrong   8. The oil spill resulted in the deaths of thousands of sea animals and

birds<u>; therefore,</u> it is not correct to say that it was only a small

shipping accident.

Extra Writing Practice

Situation: You and your wife/husband want to go somewhere for summer vacation. It should be somewhere that you and your wife/husband have not gone yet. You are on the telephone now with a travel agent. First, greet the agent and tell who you are and why you are calling. Then the agent will suggest places. You should reject a few of the places in order to make more dialogue.

Be sure to practice the connectors in this unit. For example, you might say, "No, we can't go to Australia. My wife hasn't been there yet, <u>but</u> I have" or "We'd like to go to a beach area <u>in order to</u> relax on the beach for a few days." Always underline the grammar point that you have used so the teacher can see what you are trying to practice.

Unit 11

VERB + Direct or Indirect Object

1. direct and indirect objects
2. Pattern A: VERB + PREPOSITION + object
   (group 1: *to;* group 2: *for*)
3. Pattern B: VERB + indirect object + direct object
   (group 3: no preposition)
4. Pattern A or Pattern B
   (group 4: *to;* group 5: *for*)

Grammar Words: object, direct object, indirect object

object   In conversational English, "object" means a thing. However, in
                grammar, "object" means a noun (or pronoun) after a verb. It can be
                a thing or a person. The object receives the action of the verb. There
                are two kinds of objects in English grammar.

direct object   A direct object is the thing or person that receives the action of the
                       verb.
                            I study <u>English</u>.
                            Evelyn called <u>Jamie</u> last night.
                            He put <u>the book</u> on the table.

indirect object   An indirect object is the person to whom or for whom the action
                       of the verb is done.
                            I gave <u>Mary</u> the book.
                            Please pass <u>me</u> the salt.

There are two different patterns for direct and indirect objects:

Pattern A: I gave the book to Mary.
subject + VERB + direct object + PREPOSITION + indirect object

Pattern B: I gave Mary the book.
subject + VERB + indirect object + direct object

Some verbs must use pattern A, but other verbs must use pattern B. Some other
verbs can use pattern A or pattern B. Some verbs use **to** and others use **for**. In this
lesson, we will study the five different groups of verbs for direct and indirect objects.

Pattern A:
Subject + VERB + Direct Object + PREPOSITION + Indirect Object

Group 1: **announce, explain, report, suggest, introduce, describe, mention,
speak, repeat, say**

These verbs *must* use the preposition **to.** (*Hint:* Many of these verbs involve oral
communication.)

Pattern A: I explained the lesson to Scott.
              She said hello to me.
              He introduced his cousin to me.

Group 2: **open, close, pronounce, prescribe, do, answer, change, cash**

These verbs *must* use the preposition **for.**

Pattern A: He opened the door for me.
              She did the work for me.
              The woman at the bank cashed the check for me.

Exercise 1.   Circle the letter of the correct sentences. Follow the example.

example: (A) He announced the schedule to the students.
                (B) He announced the students the schedule.

1. (A) Please open Alja the door.

   (B) Please open the door for Alja.

2. (A) They did the dishes for us.

   (B) They did us the dishes.

3. (A) Mrs. Palermo explained the lesson to the class.

   (B) Mrs. Palermo explained the class the lesson.

4. (A) The doctor prescribed me the medicine.

   (B) The doctor prescribed the medicine for me.

5. (A) He repeated me the words.

   (B) He repeated the words to me.

6. (A) The class pronounced the words for the teacher.

   (B) The class pronounced the teacher the words.

7. (A) He changed us his plans.

   (B) He changed his plans for us.

8. (A) My father mentioned the trip to the kids.

   (B) My father mentioned the kids the trip.

9. (A) Would you please open the door for the man?

   (B) Would you please open the man the door?

10. (A) Keith introduced Martha to Ali.

    (B) Keith introduced Ali Martha.

11. (A) They described me their new house.

    (B) They described their new house to me.

12. (A) He answered us the questions.

    (B) He answered the questions for us.

Exercise 2. Underline *to* or *for.* Follow the examples.

examples: describe the picture (<u>to</u>, for) me
mention the idea (<u>to</u>, for) me

1. explain the answer (to, for) him
2. answer the question (to, for) her
3. say hello (to, for) us
4. prescribe the treatment (to, for) me
5. introduce his teacher (to, for) me

6. pronounce this Greek name (to, for) me
7. speak Vietnamese (to, for) them
8. close the box (to, for) me
9. did the work (to, for) him
10. repeat the words (to, for) you

Exercise 3. Write *to me* or *for me.* Follow the example.

example: describe the house _____to me_____

1. open the door _____
2. suggest a nice restaurant_____
3. prescribe these tablets _____
4. do the work _____
5. explain this word _____

6. cash the check _____
7. say good-bye _____
8. mention your idea _____
9. answer number 1 _____
10. close the window _____

Exercise 4. Write *to* or *for* on the line. Follow the example.

example: The teacher announced the date of the test _____to_____ the students.

1. Our teacher always pronounces the new words loudly _____ us.
2. I introduced Susan _____ Shirley.
3. Could you please open the jar _____ me?
4. Srini mentioned his idea _____ his classmates.
5. She explained the vocabulary _____ the students.
6. She opened the door _____ Jane.
7. She cashed the money order _____ me.
8. I usually speak English _____ Ms. Williams.

9. The teacher repeated the answers _____ the class.

10. I described my trip to Saudi Arabia _____ my family.

11. I talked to the teacher about the test, and she changed my grade _____ me.

12. I always say hello _____ Georgia.

13. When did your coach explain the new plays _____ you?

14. The girl closed the window _____ the woman.

15. Margie reported the news _____ her friends.

16. We suggested that new restaurant _____ them.

17. I was really busy, so Renée did the grocery shopping _____ me.

18. The teacher answered the question _____ us.

19. The cashier will not cash that check _____ you if you don't have any ID.

20. What does Rick look like? Can you describe him _____ me?

Exercise 5.   Write *to* or *for* in the blanks to complete these conversations. Follow the examples.

examples: *Darrin:* Don is a really nice person.
               Betsy: Yes, he is. He always says hello __to__ everyone.

               David: Did he help you?
               Kay: Yes, he did. He explained all the chess moves __to__ me.

1. *Mark:*   I heard you have a new car. Could you describe it _____ me?

    Tina: It's a light green sports car. It's a four-door Nissan.

2. *Roxanne:* Have you heard about the party tomorrow night?

    Will: Yes, I have. Emily told me about it.

    Roxanne: Some of us are going to meet at Michelle's house first. Do you want to

                come?

    Will: Eve mentioned that _____ me. I think that might be a good idea.

3. *Amy:*   Do you know Zack? He's Phil's cousin.

    Carolyn: Yes, I do. Phil introduced Zack _____ me about a week or so ago.

4. *Kerry:* Hey, it's kind of cold in here, isn't it?

    Lori: It's getting a little chilly in here. Do you want me to close the window

    _____ you?

    Kerry: Yeah, thanks.

5. *Saul:* What did Eric get on the homework?

    Pam: He got a 100.

    Saul: 100? Are you kidding? Eric?

    Pam: Yes, Eric's grade was 100. I saw it.

    Saul: Well, I think Eric's father did the work _____ him. There's no way that

    Eric could get 100 on the homework in that class.

6. *Joshua:* Are you hungry? I'm going to go to McDonald's now. If you're interested

    in going with me, let me know.

    Wes: Thanks but no thanks. I ate dinner at Mary Kay's house.

    Joshua: Did she make dinner _____ you?

    Wes: Yes, she did. She invited Art and me, so we both ate there tonight. It was

    great.

Pattern B: Subject + VERB + Indirect Object + Direct Object

Group 3: **ask, wish, cost, save, charge**

These verbs do NOT use a preposition between the two objects.

Pattern A: Oprah wished me happy birthday.
The girl charged me too much money. It was a mistake.
He asked the teacher a hard question.

▬▬▬▬

Exercise 6.   Circle the number of the correct sentence. Follow the example.

example: (1) The man asked us the question.
(2) The man asked the question to us.

1. (1) My mother wished a good trip to us.

    (2) My mother wished us a good trip.

2. (1) That shirt cost me thirty dollars.

   (2) That shirt cost thirty dollars to me.

3. (1) That restaurant charges four dollars to its customers for coffee.

   (2) That restaurant charges its customers four dollars for coffee.

4. (1) The students asked the teacher several questions.

   (2) The students asked several questions to the teacher.

5. (1) Janet told me about the big sale. She saved a lot of money to me.

   (2) Janet told me about the big sale. She saved me a lot of money.

Exercise 7.   Write a new sentence with the words in parentheses. Follow the example.

   example: He wished a good trip. (Andrea) <u>He wished Andrea a good trip.</u>

1. He's going to ask a question. (the teacher)

   _____

2. They charged twenty dollars for a new shirt. (Mr. Hernandez)

   _____

3. She saved ten dollars by telling him about the sale at the store. (Joe)

   _____

4. We asked the time of day. (the man)

   _____

5. The old man wished a happy holiday. (us)

   _____

6. The new red bicycle cost over one hundred dollars. (me)

   _____

7. That store charged fifteen dollars for some cotton socks. (her)

   _____

8. All of us wished a safe journey. (Zoe)

   _____

Exercise 8.   Each sentence has a mistake. Find the mistake and write the correct sentence. Follow the example.

example: My grandfather wished to me a happy birthday.

<u>   My grandfather wished me a happy birthday.   </u>

1. That new dress cost for Maria seventy dollars.

_____

2. Can you ask to the pilot a question?

_____

3. How much did Sears charge to you?

_____

4. I save to myself a lot of money by not smoking.

_____

5. My uncle wished good luck to me on the test tomorrow.

_____

6. One student asked three difficult questions to the teacher yesterday.

_____

Pattern A: Subject + VERB + Direct Object + PREPOSITION + Indirect Object
OR
Pattern B: Subject + VERB + Indirect Object + Direct Object

Group 4: **give, write, read, show, teach, tell, sell, lend, bring, take, pass**

These verbs can use either pattern A or pattern B. If they use A, they use **to.**

Pattern A
I gave the book to John.
He wrote a letter to Kyoko.
They took the books to John.

Pattern B
I gave John the book.
He wrote Kyoko a letter.
They took John the books.

Group 5: **buy, get, make, find, do a favor**

These verbs can use either pattern A or pattern B. If they use A, they use **for.**

Pattern A   *Pattern B*
I bought a gift for Debbie.   I bought Debbie a gift.
He made some soup for me.   He made me some soup.
They did a favor for her.   They did her a favor.

Exercise 9.   Circle the letter of the correct answer. Follow the example.

example: (A) Pat gives the books to Ryan.
             (B) Pat gives Ryan the books.

1. (A) He is writing a letter to Gwen.

   (B) He is writing Gwen a letter.

2. (A) Pass the salt to me.

   (B) Pass me the salt.

3. (A) He showed his new suit to me.

   (B) He showed me his new suit.

4. (A) I am going to sell my car to Tabitha.

   (B) I am going to sell Tabitha my car.

5. (A) Are you taking this money to Mr. Choi?

   (B) Are you taking Mr. Choi this money?

6. (A) I bought a card for Chip.

   (B) I bought Chip a card.

7. (A) He got a chair for the new student.

   (B) He got the new student a chair.

8. (A) He made dinner for us.

   (B) He made us dinner.

9. (A) I'm happy because someone found the keys for me.

   (B) I'm happy because someone found me the keys.

10. (A) I bought a present for the cat.

    (B) I bought the cat a present.

Exercise 10.   Write a sentence with *to.* Follow the example.

example: Jo gave Ernie the baseball.

_____ Jo gave the baseball to Ernie. _____

1. Warren wrote Molly a letter.   _____

2. I always read my brother   _____

   the newspaper.

3. We show the class our artwork.   _____

4. She teaches the students   _____

   new words.

5. Please tell Rose the good news.   _____

6. I'm going to sell Daria my bike.   _____

7. I usually lend Paul my car.   _____

8. Did she bring the teacher another apple? _____

9. Would you please take your _____

   father the food?

10. He passed me the pepper. _____

Exercise 11.   Write a sentence without *to.* Follow the example.

example: Gina gives the books to Trevor.

_____ Gina gives Trevor the books. _____

1. I didn't teach golf to Kim.   _____

2. He showed the map to Diane.   _____

3. He brought some flowers to me.   _____

4. Please lend the money to Carl.   _____

5. Did you write a thank-you note   _____

   to your sister?

6. I sold my old stove to Lisa.   _____

7. Pass the test to Alan.   _____

8. She is going to read the poem   _____

   to me.

9. Take the money to Ms. Brady.   _____

10. I never tell lies to my parents.   _____

Exercise 12.   Write a sentence with *for.* Follow the example.

> *example:*   She bought Matt a ticket.

> _____ She bought a ticket for Matt. _____

1. I'm going to get Joanne some tea. _____

2. She found Andy a job.   _____

3. He made the girl a sandwich.   _____

4. The teacher got the student a pencil. _____

5. My brother did me a favor.   _____

Exercise 13.   Write a sentence without *for.* Follow the example.

> *example:*   She bought a vase for Jane.

> _____ She bought Jane a vase. _____

1. I made some coffee for the   _____

   students.

2. Mr. Erwin got some nice   _____

   flowers for his wife.

3. He found a key for me.   _____

4. They did a big favor for me.   _____

5. They didn't buy a ticket for me.   _____

Exercise 14.   Write A, B, or AB on the line to show the possible answers. Follow
the examples.

1. Travis gave __AB__.

   (A) the boxes to Gene

   (B) Gene the boxes

2. Norman asked __B__.

   (A) some questions to the fans

   (B) the fans some questions

3. He explained _____.

   (A) the lesson to me

   (B) me the lesson

4. She sent _____.

   (A) the letter to Paul

   (B) Paul the letter

5. The teacher showed _____.

   (A) the test to the boys

   (B) the boys the test

6. The shirt cost _____.

   (A) ten dollars to me

   (B) me ten dollars

7. We took _____.

   (A) the boxes to them

   (B) them the boxes

8. Gladys introduced _____.

   (A) Naren to me

   (B) me to Naren

9. We usually speak _____.

   (A) Spanish to him

   (B) him Spanish

10. I mentioned _____.

    (A) the idea to him

    (B) him the idea

11. I wrote _____.

    (A) an e-mail message to him

    (B) him an e-mail message

12. We told _____.

    (A) the news to them

    (B) them the news

13. Gary repeated _____.

    (A) the sentence to us

    (B) us the sentence

14. They described _____.

    (A) their trip to us

    (B) us their trip

15. She bought _____.

    (A) their lunch for them

    (B) them their lunch

16. That store charged _____.

    (A) ten dollars to us

    (B) us ten dollars

17. Sam and Laura taught _____.

    (A) the verbs to me

    (B) me the verbs

18. We reported _____.

    (A) the news to my father

    (B) my father the news

19. The woman is reading _____.

    (A) the story to the kids

    (B) the kids the story

20. Who suggested _____?

    (A) that restaurant to you

    (B) you that restaurant

Exercise 15. Write A, B, or AB to show the possible answers.
Follow the example.

1. He pronounced ___A___.

   (A) the words for me

   (B) me the words

2. The doctor prescribed _____.

   (A) the medicine for me

   (B) me the medicine

3. We made _____.

   (A) the reservation for them

   (B) them the reservation

4. Who did _____?

   (A) the dishes for you

   (B) you the dishes

5. We got _____.

   (A) some tickets for the students

   (B) the students some tickets

6. I found _____.

   (A) a chair for him

   (B) him a chair

7. I opened _____.

   (A) the door for him

   (B) him the door

8. I am going to find _____.

   (A) the map for you

   (B) you the map

9. Please do _____.

   (A) a favor for me

   (B) me a favor

10. Would you please close _____?

    (A) the window for us

    (B) us the window

11. She's going to buy _____.

    (A) a new scarf for you

    (B) you a new scarf

12. They changed _____.

    (A) their plans for me

    (B) me their plans

Exercise 16. Write *to me, for me,* or *me* on the line. Follow the examples.

   examples: He gave the watch _____to me_____.

   He gave _____me_____ the watch.

1. He repeated the words _____.

2. He bought _____ the tie.

3. He answered the questions

   _____.

4. Please pronounce these words

   _____.

5. They spoke German _____.

6. Please tell _____ the answer.

7. Pass the salt _____.

8. He's going to read the story _____.

9. The travel agent made a reservation

_____.

10. They explained the answer

_____.

11. He wrote _____ a long letter.

12. He said hello _____.

13. She opened the door _____.

14. He bought the tie _____

_____.

15. He described his trip _____.

16. He wished _____ a good trip.

17. She got _____ a nice present.

18. He gave _____ a new shirt.

19. He finally found a chair _____.

20. He's getting a chair _____.

21. He's getting _____ a chair.

22. She made a small cake _____.

23. She's making _____ a cake.

24. He didn't lend _____ $100.

CHALLENGE   In English, these sentences are correct.

    I gave Jerry the money.
    I made Elaine some homemade pasta.
However, these sentences follow the same word order but are wrong.
    I gave him it.
    I made her it.
Why do you think these last two sentences are not correct? The word order is the same as in the first two. What is the grammar rule here?

Exercise 17.   Write the correct verb on the line. Follow the example.

        example: Tim _____*gave*_____ the present to me.
                (gave, bought, opened)

1. The teacher _____ the question to me. (asked, answered, explained)

2. He _____ a chocolate pie for me. (gave, made, described)

3. I am going to _____ my new car to them. (save, show, change)

4. My sister always _____ long letters to me. (finds, sends, answers)

5. Please _____ me the salt. (open, pass, repeat)

6. Laken and Kyle _____ the words for me. (explained, repeated, pronounced)

7. Did Brenda _____ the books to them? (find, take, close)

8. Mr. Ismail _____ ten dollars to Barney. (sent, saved, charged)

9. Did the doctor _____ the medicine to you? (buy, bring, prescribe)

10. My parents did not _____ me a new bicycle. (get, change, suggest)

11. I often _____ money to Pablo. (lend, change, charge)

12. They _____ it for us. (found, wished, explained)

13. Melinda usually _____ me hello. (says, tells, speaks)

14. She _____ me a very fun and safe trip. (said, wished, described)

15. He _____ the idea to my class. (made, asked, mentioned)

16. We're going to _____ her a silver watch. (open, give, describe)

Speaking Activity
((( ))))

Exercise 18.   Speaking Activity

Step 1.   Do student A OR student B. Do <u>one</u> of these only.

Step 2.   Number the left lines from 1 to 8 in any order. Mix up the numbers.

Step 3.   Read the words. Write the correct combination. Add *to* or *for* if it's neces-sary.   Sometimes there are two possible answers. Write both. When you have finished, check your answers with another student who did the same part (A or B) as you did.

Step 4.   Work with a partner who did not do the same part as you. Student A will read out all eight items as quickly as possible in numerical order. Student B must close the book and listen and then complete the items correctly. For example, student A will say, "give / a CD / me" and student B must say, "give me a CD" and "give a CD to me" because there are two answers. If this is correct, student A says, "That's correct." If this is not correct, student A says, "Try again" and repeats the item. When all the items are finished, student B will read out his or her eight items.

examples: give / a CD / me

_____ give a CD to me _____

_____ give me a CD _____

ask / a question / the teacher

_____ ask the teacher a question _____

_____

answer / me / a question

_____ answer a question for me _____

_____

Student A

____. buy / Sammy / a gift

_____

_____

____. explain / me / the new word

_____

_____

____. introduce / her / me

_____

_____

____. wish / happy birthday / Sandy

_____

_____

____. say / me / hello

_____

_____

____. give / the cards / me

_____

_____

____. show / my new computer / them

_____

_____

____. close / the door / me

_____

_____

Student B

____. do / the work / us

_____

_____

____. make / a cake / me

_____

_____

____. wish / good luck / us

_____

_____

____. describe / me / your new house

_____

_____

____. explain / us / the directions

_____

_____

____. open / me / the door

_____

_____

____. take / these books / Mr. Lee

_____

_____

____. find / the girl / a chair

_____

_____

Exercise 19.   Multiple Choice. Circle the letter of the correct answer.

1. *Rich:*   "Did you hear the news yesterday?"

    Austin: "Yes, I did. That man announced _____."

    (A) it us   (C) it to us

    (B) us it   (D) it for us

2. She didn't have her key, so Sharmista opened _____.

    (A) her the door   (C) the door for her

    (B) her for the door   (D) the door her

3. She is a very friendly person. She always _____ every day.

    (A) says everyone hello   (C) tell everyone hello

    (B) says hello to everyone   (D) tell hello everyone

4. Nurses know a lot about medicine, but they can't prescribe _____.

    (A) patients any medicine   (C) any medicine to patients

    (B) any medicine patients   (D) any medicine for patients

5. My sister _____ it for me.

    (A) gave   (C) wished

    (B) found   (D) explained

6. *Kate:*   "Did you understand the word?"

    Kristen: "Yes, I did. Mr. Julius _____ it to me."

    (A) asked   (C) answered

    (B) explained   (D) pronounced

7. Please give this telegram _____.

    (A) to her   (C) for her

    (B) at her   (D) her

8. Please do _____. Can you lend me $10 until tomorrow?

    (A) a favor to me   (C) a favor for me

    (B) a favor me   (D) for a favor me

Exercise 20.   Review Test

Part 1.   Read these sentences. Fill in the blanks with *to, for,* or —.

1. My parents bought _____ me a large suitcase when I went to France. They gave it

    _____ me a week before I left.

2. *Brent:*   Hey, your car is a different color!

    Craig: Do you like it? I decided to change the color.

    Brent: Did you paint it?

    Craig: No, I didn't. I took it to a shop on West Street. It's called Car Colors.

    Brent: How much did they charge _____ you?

    Craig: It cost _____ me about $300.

    Brent: Wow, that was a good price. And your car looks great!

3. Ms. Carlisle is an excellent teacher. She speaks _____ the students very slowly. If

    they do not understand something, she repeats the information _____ the

    students.   She pronounces all the new words _____ the students very carefully

    and clearly. Students are not afraid to ask _____ her a question. Ms. Carlisle can

    usually answer any question _____ us very easily.

4. I didn't have my key with me, so Joseph opened the door _____ me.

Part 2.   Circle the correct word.

1. I often (lend, change, charge) money to Al.

2. He (made, asked, mentioned) the idea to me and my friends.

3. Please (open, pass, describe) me the salt.

4. Sharon usually (says, tells, speaks) me hello.

Part 3.   Read each sentence carefully. Look at the underlined part. If the under-
            lined part is correct, circle the word *correct*. If it is wrong, circle the wrong
            part and write the correct form above.

correct   wrong   1. I asked <u>the location to the police officer</u>.

correct   wrong   2. Please take <u>these boxes to Kevin</u>.

correct   wrong   3. Ed <u>showed us his new car</u> yesterday.

correct   wrong   4. My father bought a present <u>to me</u> because I passed the test.

correct   wrong   5. Who <u>told to you the news about Laura</u>?

Extra Writing Practice

Situation: Write a dialogue that takes place in a department store. A few days ago you bought a present for your cousin. However, you found out that your cousin already has this gift, so you want to return it. However, the clerk does not want to allow you to return the gift. You can choose any kind of gift that you want. Make up something interesting or strange or funny to add to the dialogue.

Be sure to practice several of the verb and object combinations from this unit. For example, you might say, "I <u>bought</u> this shirt <u>for</u> my cousin, but I can't <u>give</u> it <u>to</u> him because he already has this kind of shirt." Always underline the grammar point that you have used so the teacher can see what you are trying to practice.

Unit 12

Review

1. phrasal verbs
2. past progressive tense
3. present perfect tense
4. adverbs of manner and related terms
5. verb-preposition and adjective-preposition combinations
6. passive voice
7. relative clauses
8. infinitives and gerunds
9. connectors
10. verbs with direct or indirect objects

Exercise 1. Phrasal Verbs. Write a short answer for the question in which you repeat the phrasal verb and add the appropriate object pronoun. Follow the example.

1. Did Steve pick up his sister at the airport?   Yes, he _____*picked her up*_____.

2. Did they really give away a new car?   Yes, they _____.

3. Did the teacher go over the quiz?   Yes, she _____.

4. Have you already handed in your paper?   Yes, I _____.

5. Did you run into Maureen and Marcia at the mall?   Yes, I _____.

6. Did you run out of milk?   Yes, we _____.

7. Did you come across my watch?   Yes, I _____.

8. Are you looking after your baby brother?   Yes, I _____.

9. Are you counting on Tracy and Chris for help?   Yes, we _____.

10. Has he filled out the application already?   Yes, he _____.

11. Can someone turn on the lights?   Yes, I'll _____.

12. Does your teacher call on you a lot?   Yes, he _____ all the time.

Exercise 2. Simple Past vs. Past Progressive. Write the correct form of the verb in parentheses. Use simple past or past progressive tense.

1. When I (wait) _____ for the bus, it started to rain.

2. After I (eat) _____ my dinner last night, I (write) _____ a letter of complaint to the telephone company.

3. I (wake) _____ up because the dogs outside (bark) _____.

4. When (arrive) _____ you _____ here?

5. *Anna:* Did you feel the earthquake last night?

   Carol: Yes, I did. I (sleep) _____ when it (hit) _____.

   Anna: So what (do) _____ you _____?

   Carol: I (jump) _____ out of bed and (put) _____ on my

      bathrobe.

6. I couldn't leave my house this morning because it (rain) _____ so hard. I

   (have) _____ to wait for about fifteen minutes before I was able to go

   out.

7. I (get) _____ home at 7 P.M. My son (play) _____ in the

   backyard, and my daughter (watch) _____ TV. I (get) _____

   angry because they (do) _____ their homework then.

8. *Fred:* I just (see) _____ Martin. He (ride) _____ his

      bike by the post office.

   Jerry: When I (see) _____ him last week, he (do) _____

      the same thing.

Exercise 3. Present Perfect Tense. Underline the correct verb tense. Sometimes more than one answer is possible. Be prepared to explain the reason for your choices.

1. *Liz:* How long (have you worked, did you work) at the hospital?

   Judy: Well, let's see. I (have been, was) there from 1996 to 1998, so two years.

2. *Greg:* (Did you ever go, Have you ever gone) to a professional baseball game?

   Barry: Well, I (went, have gone) to lots of pro baseball games with my dad when I (was, have been) a little kid. Why do you ask?

   Greg: I (have gone, went) to see a game last night.

Barry: How (has it been, was it)?

Greg: I (have had, had) a great time there. I think I'd like to go again, and I was

            wondering if you might like to go with me the next time I go.

3. Barbara: There's a good movie playing at the Brentwood Cinema. Do you want to

                go?

    Kathy: What's playing?

    Barbara: It's called *A Day to Remember*.

    Kathy: Oh, I (already saw, have already seen) it.

    Barbara: Really? Well, (have you liked, did you like) it? How (was it, has it been)?

    Kathy: I (have thought, thought) that it (was, has been) terrific. If I had some free

                time tonight, I'd go see it again with you, but I can't. Sorry. But you've

                really got to go see it!

4. Lynn: Do you know someone named Kelly Hall?

    Rick: Yes, I do. I (knew, have known) her for about five or six years.

    Lynn: Really? How (have you met, did you meet) her?

    Rick: I think it was at a company dinner.

Exercise 4.   Underline the correct words.

1. The (beautiful, beautifully) little child surprised us (by pick, by picking, with pick,

    with picking) up the spiders without any fear.

2. Everyone agreed that the basketball coach made a (smart, smartly) decision to take

    Patrick out of the game because he was not playing so (good, well).

3. Jack: How did you get in the house? I thought you lost your key.

    Scott: Well, I was able to get into the house (with, by) another key that I had.

4. By (open, opening) the door (slow, slowly), he was able to keep the cat from getting

    out of the house.

5. The best way (by get, by getting, to get, to getting) a high score on the vocabulary test is to write an original sentence with each word.

6. *Luke:* This package has to be in Ann Arbor by tomorrow evening.

 Jeff: You can send it (by, with) overnight delivery.

 Luke: Will that cost a lot of money?

 Jeff: It's not the cheapest method, but (by, with) using that kind of service, you can be sure that your package will be there by tomorrow evening.

Exercise 5. Verb-Preposition and Adjective-Preposition Combinations. Write the missing prepositions on the lines.

1. I think this sweater belongs _____ Terry. At first, I thought it might be Karen's, but it's different _____ the sweater that Karen was wearing at dinner tonight.

2. Does anyone know what happened _____ my keys? They were right here and now they're gone. Could someone help me to look _____ them? I am really tired _____ working all day, and I just want to find my keys and go home.

3. My mother doesn't approve _____ my friends. She always complains _____ them. I am so tired _____ listening _____ her complaints!

4. Tennis is my favorite sport. I'm just crazy _____ it. No matter how much work I have to do, I'm always ready _____ a match. Although I haven't been very success-ful _____ any tennis tournaments, I always look forward _____ a good match.

5. If you slip on a banana peel in a restaurant, is the restaurant responsible _____ the accident? I mean, is the restaurant guilty _____ any kind of crime or negligence?

Exercise 6.   Passive Voice. Underline the correct verb form.

1. *Jacob:*   If I (am wanted, want) to study English at this school, what should I (do, be

    done)?

    Alan: First, an application must (complete, be completed). A deposit of $200

    should (include, be included) with the application.

    Jacob: OK, so if I (fill, am filled) this out right now, can you (help, be helped) me?

    Alan: Sure. Let's do it.

    Jacob: Should this form (fill, be filled) out in pen or pencil?

    Alan: Pen (prefers, is preferred), but you can (use, be used) pencil, too.

2. *Margo:*   Don't do that! It's bad luck.

    Danny: What are you talking about?

    Margo: In my country, opening an umbrella indoors (considers, is

    considered) bad luck.

    Danny: Really? Well, in my country, we (don't like, aren't liked) to get

    wet in the rain!

3. *Miles:*   What languages (speak, are spoken) in Switzerland?

    Tina: German (speaks, is spoken) by people in the northern, central, and eastern

    parts of   the country.

    Irene: What about French? I think that a lot of people in the western part of the

    country (speak, are spoken, is spoken) French.

    Nancy: And don't forget that Italian (speaks, spoke, is spoken, was spoken) in the

    southern part of the country.

    Tina: Oh, and don't forget Romansh. It's one of the four national languages, too.

4. *Hank:*   Hey, my paycheck is less than it was last month.

    Paula: Yes, that's correct. Starting this month, an extra five percent of your salary

    (takes, is taken) out for the new retirement plan.

    Hank: Five percent? Gosh, that's a lot. Let me see if my check (has calculated, has

    been calculated) correctly.

    Paula: Well, is it right?

    Hank: Yes, it is. They (have done, have been done) it correctly.

Exercise 7.   Relative Clauses. Fill in the blanks with *who, whom, that, which,* or
—. If more than one answer is possible, list ALL possible answers
to demonstrate your full knowledge of relative clauses.

1. *Jerry:*   What have you been up to?

   Patty: I just came back from Dimes and Dollars.

   Jerry: Dimes and Dollars? What's that?

   Patty: It's that new department store (1) _____ is on the corner of Fowler
   and Cleveland.

   Jerry: What were you doing there? Shopping?

   Patty: Actually, no. I wanted to return something (2) _____ I bought
   last week.

   Jerry: And were you able to return it?

   Patty: At first, the clerk didn't want to give me a refund, so she called the manager
   (3) _____ was on duty. He was reluctant to give me my money back, so
   I just pointed to the huge sign (4) _____ is right there behind the
   register. It clearly says, "We refund all items (5) _____ you have
   purchased within the last 30 days as long as you have the sales receipt."

   Jerry: And did you have the sales receipt?

   Patty: Yes, but the receipt (6) _____ I had was 29 days old, so the clerk didn't
   know if I could get my money back.

   Jerry: Maybe the clerk (7) _____ you spoke to was new or just didn't know
   the rules for exchanges.

2. *Trina:*   What have you got there?

   Nathan: These are pictures (8) _____ I just picked up from the photo shop.

   Trina: How did they turn out?

   Nathan: Well, I had three rolls of film (9) _____ I took to the shop. The pictures
   (10) _____ turned out the best are the ones (11) _____ I took last
   summer when we all went canoeing on the river. Do you remember
   that day?

Trina: Yes, I certainly do. I had such a good time that day.

Nathan: But the other two rolls didn't turn out great. In fact, the pictures from the

             roll (12) _____ had pictures of my birthday party are just about useless.

             They're just not clear enough.

Exercise 8.   Infinitives and Gerunds. Fill in the blanks with the correct form of
                    the verb in parentheses.

My friend Melissa offered (1. take) _____ me out for dinner last night, so

I decided to take her up on her offer.* I don't get invited (2. eat) _____ out a

lot, so I couldn't help (3. take) _____ advantage of this opportunity for a free

meal and some pleasant company. Melissa is an office executive and has a pretty good

salary, so she is accustomed to (4. eat) _____ out at really nice restaurants. I,

on the other hand, have a part-time job at the supermarket, so if I eat out, I prefer (5. go)

_____ to a cheap place. In fact, when Melissa invited me (6. eat)

_____ dinner with her, I suggested (7. go) _____ to an inexpen-

sive restaurant, but she insisted on (8. take) _____ me to a really nice place.

Melissa ordered the most expensive item on the menu. I wanted (9. get)

_____ a tuna fish sandwich, but she persuaded me (10. order)

_____ something more expensive.

   "A tuna fish sandwich?" she asked in a slightly surprised tone. "Do you expect me (11.

believe) _____ that you don't want (12. eat) _____ lobster? This

restaurant is famous for its lobster, not its tuna fish sandwiches. What can I do in order to

get you (13. change) _____ your mind?" It only took a little bit of friendly

pressure from Melissa to convince me (14. order) _____ lobster from the

menu. In fact, (15. listen) _____ to Melissa's friendly suggestion was definitely

the correct thing to do. The lobster was out of this world.**

*to take someone up on his/her offer = to accept that person's invitation or offer to do something for you
**be out of this world = be very good, be terrific

Exercise 9.   Connectors. Underline the correct answers to complete these sentences.

1. The word "green" has two vowels in it, and (too, so, either, neither) ("bread" does, does "bread," "bread" has, has "bread").

2. She bought some new shoes (for, to, so) match her new dress.

3. The snow started just as the game was about to begin. (So, Therefore, However), the game was postponed until tomorrow.

4. It didn't rain last Monday, and it didn't rain the Monday before that (too, so, either, neither).

5. He went to the hardware store, so he (got, needs to get) some nails.

6. Each state has two senators in Congress. There are fifty states. (Therefore, However), there are one hundred senators.

7. Jackie didn't bring her passport, and I didn't (so, too, either, neither).

8. She bought an extra bag of potatoes (in order, for, so, to) make enough potato salad for all the people who were coming to dinner that night.

9. I (wanted, didn't want) to do any of the housework, and neither did Shirley.

10. I looked up all of the thirty vocabulary words and wrote down the meanings, and so (was, did, may, might) Phil.

11. Sherry's kids hate onions. Grandmother put onions in the beans that she cooked, (but, so, for, to) Sherry's kids refused to eat the beans.

12. A koala bear is a mammal, and (so is, so are, is so, are so) a kangaroo.

13. I am crazy about doing crossword puzzles, but my husband (does, is, doesn't, isn't).

14. Gwen (speaks, speak, can speak, can't speak) Spanish and Greek, and so can Belinda.

15. They've already cleaned their bedrooms, (and so I have, but I haven't, so I have too).

Exercise 10.   VERB + Direct/Indirect Objects. Write *to, for,* or — on the line.

1. Pedro introduced his cousin _____ us.

2. The doctor prescribed a strict diet _____ me.

3. Would you please open the door _____ me?

4. How come she speaks English _____ her mom but French _____ her dad?

5. If you don't like the company's decision, you can write a letter _____ the president.

6. She said good-bye _____ everyone and then boarded the train.

7. It was her birthday, so we all bought _____ her a gift.

8. I sold my skis _____ her because I was returning to my country and didn't need them any more.

9. I explained all of the steps _____ him, but he still didn't get it.

10. I'm a little busy right now. I have to take _____ Debra these files.

11. When I was sick, Melinda did all of this work _____ me.

12. I've never been to Scotland. Could you describe the scenery _____ me?

Exercise 11.   VERB + Direct/Indirect Objects. Four of these sentences have an error with direct/indirect objects. Circle the errors and write the correct form above.

1. When my shoes get too small for me, I usually give them to Courtney.

2. Could you please pass for me the salt?

3. She always says hello to everyone who passes by her.

4. Today my boss finally introduced her husband to us.

5. I like his class. He always pronounces the new words very clearly for the students.

6. I didn't have my watch, so I asked the time to Nick.

7. Hey, it's a little cool in here. Could you please close the windows for me?

8. All of us sang "Happy Birthday" to wish good luck to Sarah on her new year.

9. I'd like to ask you a question if you have enough time right now.

10. I'm going to get some tea to us now. I'll be right back.

Extra Writing Practice

Situation: A friend has written you a letter in which he asks you for advice about learning English. Write him a letter. Try to give as many pieces of advice as possible about the best way to learn English. Try to include some suggestions that you have actually used successfully to help you learn English. If you want, you may also include suggestions that some people gave you that didn't work for you.

Be sure to practice several of the grammar items in this review unit. For example, you might say, "I <u>was interested in</u> improving my speaking ability, <u>so</u> I <u>tried to talk</u> to as many native speakers as possible." Always underline the grammar point that you have used so the teacher can see what you are trying to practice.

Appendix of Irregular Past and Past Participles

be	was/were	been	hang	hung	hung
become	became	become	have	had	had
begin	began	begun	hide	hid	hidden
bend	bent	bent	hit	hit	hit
bind	bound	bound	hold	held	held
bite	bit	bitten	hurt	hurt	hurt
bleed	bled	bled			
blow	blew	blown	keep	kept	kept
break	broke	broken	know	knew	known
bring	brought	brought			
build	built	built	lead	led	led
buy	bought	bought	leave	left	left
			lend	lent	lent
catch	caught	caught	let	let	let
choose	chose	chosen	lie	lay	lain
come	came	come	lose	lost	lost
cost	cost	cost			
cut	cut	cut	make	made	made
			mean	meant	meant
deal	dealt	dealt	meet	met	met
dig	dug	dug			
drink	drank	drunk	put	put	put
drive	drove	driven			
do	did	done	read	read	read
draw	drew	drawn	ride	rode	ridden
			ring	rang	rung
eat	ate	eaten	run	ran	run
fall	fell	fallen	say	said	said
feed	fed	fed	see	saw	seen
feel	felt	felt	seek	sought	sought
fight	fought	fought	sell	sold	sold
find	find	find	send	sent	sent
fly	flew	flown	set	set	set
forget	forgot	forgotten	shake	shook	shaken
freeze	froze	frozen	shoot	shot	shot
			show	showed	shown
get	got	gotten	shrink	shrank	shrunk
give	gave	given	sing	sang	sung
go	went	gone	sink	sank	sunk
grow	grew	grown	sit	sat	sat

sleep	slept	slept
slide	slid	slid
speak	spoke	spoken
spend	spent	spent
stand	stood	stood
steal	stole	stolen
strike	struck	struck
swear	swore	sworn
sweep	swept	swept
swim	swam	swum
swing	swung	swung
take	took	taken
teach	taught	taught
tear	tore	torn
tell	told	told
think	thought	thought
throw	threw	thrown
understand	understood	understood
wake	woke	woken
wear	wore	worn
win	won	won
wind	wound	wound
wring	wrung	wrung
write	wrote	written

Answer Key

Unit 1

Ex. 1, p. 1: 1. a 2. a 3. the 4. the 5. the 6. — 7. — 8. a 9. the 10. the 11. — 12. the 13. — 14. the 15. the 16. the 17. — 18. the 19. the 20. the 21. the 22. — 23. — 24. the 25. the 26. — 27. — 28. — 29. the 30. the 31. — 32. The 33. — 34. — 35. the 36. the 37. the 38. a 39. the 40. — 41. —42. — 43. a 44. — 45. the

Ex. 2, p. 3: 1. the 2. the 3. — 4. — 5. — 6. the 7. the 8. the 9. — 10. the 11. the 12. — 13. the 14. — 15. the 16. the 17. — 18. the 19. the 20. the 21. — 22. — 23. — 24. — 25. the 26. the 27. the 28. — 29. the 30. —

Ex. 3, p. 3: 1. are playing, is going to play, plays 2. did, am going to do, am doing 3. is going to go, goes, went 4. did you eat, do you eat, are you going to eat 5. am studying, study, studied

Ex. 4, p. 4: 1. went 2. is going to rain 3. is watching 4. are going to be 5. give 6. take 7. am going to need 8. drew

Ex. 5, p. 5: 1. became 2. sent 3. broke 4. brought 5. built 6. sat 7. hurt 8. chose 9. left 10. drank 11. took 12. fell 13. found 14. forgot 15. wore 16. sold 17. had 18. heard 19. sang 20. held 21. bought 22. slept 23. knew 24. let 25. lost 26. tore 27. thought 28. flew 29. ran 30. saw

Ex. 6, p. 5: 1. many 2. far 3. big 4. big 5. high 6. much 7. long 8. often 9. much 10. old

Ex. 7, p. 6: 1. never study, is always 2. often 3. hardly has, always makes 4. eat 5. often 6. usually walked 7. Does Mark ever 8. isn't ever, is always 9. played baseball together all of the time 10. usually

Ex. 8, p. 7: 1. In fact, I expected HIM to win . . . 2. I have a newspaper article that shows HIM with . . . 3. I know that HE is a very good skier . . .

Ex. 9, p. 7: 1. A; *another* is singular; use *other* 2. A; use *one* to replace *a* + NOUN; change *it* to *one* 3. B; *other* is plural; change *other* to *another* 4. B; *other* is plural; change *other* to *another* 5. A; *other one* is not English; change *other* to *another* 6. A; *other* is plural; change *other* to *another* 7. B; *one* is general, *it* is specific; change *one* to *it* 8. A; *another* can't be used with *ones*, and *the* can't be used with *another;* change *another* to *other*

Ex. 10, p. 8: 1. C 2. A 3. B 4. C 5. B 6. A 7. D 8. D

Ex. 11, p. 10: 1. Los Angeles is bigger than Paris. 2. Los Angeles is the biggest city in the U.S. 3. Paris is older than Los Angeles. 4. Brazil is the largest country in South America. 5. This car is more expensive than that car. 6. August is the hottest month of the year. 7. A diamond is the hardest mineral on earth.

8. English is harder to learn than Spanish. (OR Spanish is harder to learn than English.)

Ex. 12, p. 10: 1. than 2. worse 3. bigger, the biggest 4. than, delicious 5. farther 6. the fastest 7. better 8. saltier 9. answers may vary (possible: brightest, largest, biggest) 10. the

Ex. 13, p. 11: 1. Could, must 2. can, Could, should, will, must 3. might, could, must, could, Can, would, might, can

Ex. 14, p. 12: 1. Could you help me? 2. I won't go to the party Friday night. 3. In 1995, I was able to graduate from high school. 4. Could I borrow your car tomorrow? 5. If I had a problem now, I would talk to Sallie. 6. The total should be $5.80. 7. Every driver must have a valid license. 8. You ought to call the store before you drive there. 9. Reading class is easy, so I don't have to study for it. 10. Tom may be at school, but I'm not sure.

Ex. 15, p. 13: 1. has 2. is 3. too 4. very 5. too 6. there are 7. has 8. are 9. are 10. don't have, they have 11. Most 12. almost 13. for 14. to 15. are, have, Most

Unit 2

Ex. 1, p. 18: 1. G 2. O 3. J 4. A 5. H 6. I 7. D 8. E 9. F 10. C 11. L 12. P 13. N 14. K 15. B 16. M

Ex. 2, p. 19: 1. G 2. I 3. H 4. O 5. M 6. B 7. A 8. C 9. F 10. E 11. N 12. J 13. P 14. D 15. L 16. K

Ex. 3, p. 19: 1. up, up, back or away 2. out, on, up, up 3. off, in, down 4. out, in, out, up

Ex. 4, p. 21: 1. Look them up. 2. She called him back. 3. Please write it down. 4. She tore it up. 5. Don't turn it on now. 6. He handed them out. 7. I left them out. 8. Did you fill it out? 9. Why did you leave her out? 10. She called it off.

Ex. 5, p. 23: 1. off, in 2. out of, out of 3. on, up with 4. up with, over, on 5. on, after, into 6. out for

Ex. 6, p. 23: 1. We ran out of it. 2. She put up with them. 3. They're counting on us. 4. I came across them. 5. The teacher went over it. 6. I couldn't catch up with them. 7. The professor called on him. 8. I'm looking after him. 9. We ran into them. 10. Before my presentation, I went over them.

Ex. 7 p. 24: 1. up 2. on 3. on 4. down 5. out 6. on 7. up 8. off 9. up 10. up 11. up 12. up 13. up 14. off 15. on 16. down

Ex. 8, p. 25: 1. down, up 2. off, up, on 3. on, out, on 4. off, up, up 5. up, down 6. up, on

Ex. 9, p. 26: 1. handed them in 2. C 3. counting on her 4. gave them away 5. come across this article 6. catch up with them 7. broke down (omit *it*) 8. threw them out (*batteries* is plural) 9. C 10. C

Ex. 10, p. 27:

¹t	o		²o		³u		⁴y
h		⁵c	o	⁶n	t	i	n	u	e
r			u	e		d		s
⁸o	r		t	⁹a	r	e		
u				¹⁰e	r	r		¹¹o
g		¹²i				¹³s	u	m
¹⁴h	¹⁵a	n	d	e	d		t		i
	w				¹⁶w	a	i	t
¹⁷c	a	l	l	o	¹⁸n		n	
	y				o		¹⁹d	i	e

Ex. 11, p. 29: 1. B 2. A 3. D 4. B 5. C 6. A 7. A 8. D

Ex. 12, p. 30: Part 1. 1. out, on, up, off, off, up, off 2. in, in, down, on, up, into; Part 2. 1. wrong; got through with it 2. wrong; take off (omit *it*) 3. correct 4. wrong; count on her 5. correct 6. correct 7. wrong; left them out 8. wrong; putting it off

Unit 3

Ex. 1, p. 36: 1. I ate, I was eating 2. he did, he was doing 3. they asked, they were asking 4. she took, she was taking 5. we watched, we were watching 6. it got, it was getting 7. I made, I was making 8. he began, he was beginning

Ex. 2, p. 36: 1. was making, arrived, stopped, left 2. were doing, was attending 3. was listening, didn't know, wrote 4. met, got, went, was going 5. started, went, warmed, began, was enjoying

Ex. 3, p. 37: 1. read 2. was reading 3. was reading 4. was studying 5. studied 6. studied 7. played 8. were playing 9. Was . . . playing 10. had 11. was having 12. Did . . . have, had

Ex. 4, p. 38: 1. While we were playing tennis, it began to rain. 2. While he was talking on the phone, I cut up the onions. (OR I was cutting up the onions.) 3. when I woke up this morning, it was raining. 4. When he read the news, he started to cry.

Ex. 5, p. 39: Answers will vary.

Ex. 6, p. 41: Answers will vary.

Ex. 7, p. 41: 1. B 2. B 3. D 4. C 5. A 6. A 7. B 8. C

Ex. 8, p. 43: Part 1. 1. became 2. shot 3. put, was baking, finished 4. took, were waiting 5. plugged, was watching; Part 2. 1. correct 2. wrong; were you watching 3. wrong; lived (OR: was living) 4. correct 5. wrong; happened

Unit 4

Ex. 1, p. 48: 1. been 2. made 3. forgotten 4. shown (OR showed) 5. sat 6. hit 7. stolen 8. taken 9. told 10. thought 11. lost 12. seen 13. frozen 14. sung 15. slept 16. left 17. swum 18. taught 19. broken 20. run

Ex. 2, p. 48: 1. said 2. worn 3. written 4. begun 5. ridden 6. spoken 7. bought 8. caught 9. drunk 10. eaten 11. chosen 12. won 13. become 14. brought 15. come 16. spent 17. put 18. met 19. driven 20. fallen

Ex. 3, p. 49: 1. felt 2. found 3. sold 4. held 5. kept 6. cost 7. let 8. gotten 9. gone 10. built 11. done 12. lent 13. sent 14. read 15. known 16. cut 17. flown 18. given 19. had 20. understood

Ex. 4, p. 49: 1. drive, drove, driven; ride, rode, ridden; write, wrote, written 2. catch, caught, caught; teach, taught, taught 3. cost; cut; let; put; read; hit (*read* has a pronunciation change though the spelling is the same) 4. eat, ate, eaten; fall, fell, fallen; take, took, taken 5. speak, spoke, spoken; freeze, froze, frozen; steal, stole, stolen 6. bring, brought, brought; buy, bought, bought; think, thought, thought 7. begin, began, begun; drink, drank, drunk; sing, sang, sung; swim, swam, swum 8. become, became, become; come, came, come; run, ran, run 9. drive, drove, driven; see, saw, seen; show, showed, shown; give, gave, given; know, knew, known; take, took, taken

Ex. 5, p. 51: go: I have gone, you have gone, they have gone, he has gone, Lim has gone; work: you have worked, he has worked, I have worked, she has worked, it has worked; do: I have done, you have done, we have done, he has done, they have done; be: he has been, I have been, you have been, Jill has been, Jill and I have been

Ex. 6, p. 51: 1. he has gone, he hasn't gone, has he gone? 2. I have made, I haven't made, have I made? 3. they have spoken, they haven't spoken, have they spoken? 4. you have put, you haven't put, have you put? 5. you have sung, you haven't sung, have you sung? 6. we have done, we haven't done, have we done? 7. she has thought, she hasn't thought, has she thought? 8. Ken has flown, Ken hasn't flown, has Ken flown? 9. Zina has worked, Zina hasn't worked, has Zina worked? 10. I have written, I haven't written, have I written?

Ex. 7, p. 52: Answers will vary.

Challenge, p. 52: Number 4 is not usual in North American English. When *have* is the main verb, the negative is formed with *don't* or *doesn't*. When *have* is an auxiliary verb, the negative is formed with *haven't* or *hasn't*.

Ex. 8, p. 53: 1. 've just cooked, 've just finished 2. 've just come 3. 's just run 4. 's just taken, 've just realized

Ex. 9, p. 55: 1. Have you ever eaten, 've never heard 2. Have you ever studied, Have you ever had, have you ever been (OR traveled), 've never traveled 3. Have you ever thought, 've never had

Ex. 10, p. 55: Answers will vary.

Ex. 11, p. 57: 1. since 2. for 3. since 4. since 5. for 6. since 7. for 8. since 9. for 10. for 11. since 12. since

Ex. 12, p. 57: 1. Apples have been on sale since Monday. 2. Yolanda has owned a BMW since 1997. 3. We have known the mayor for ten years. 4. I have worked at this office for two years. 5. Henry has had a huge house since he moved here. 6. Keith has played tennis since 1982. 7. Mrs. deMontluzin has taught French since 1991. 8. Dr. Lorraine has been a university professor since the fall of 1995.

Challenge, p. 58: I began to work here in 1994. I have worked here since 1994. I have worked here for (this year minus 1994) years. The important thing to note is that the verb *begin* cannot continue (because you only begin something one time), so we can't say, "I have begun this job for three years." It is illogical.

Ex. 13, p. 59: 1. Ben hasn't eaten dinner yet. 2. It hasn't rained yet. 3. The plane hasn't arrived (OR landed) yet. 4. The stew isn't finished (OR done) yet. 5. I haven't spoken with Dr. Adams yet. 6. I haven't bought my ticket yet.

Ex. 14, p. 60: Answers will vary.

Challenge, p. 61: When we say, "It's the first job that I've really liked," we are connecting all the past jobs to the present job, so we use present perfect because present perfect connects a past event and the present. However, when we say, "The first job that I liked was my job at IBM," we are talking only about that past job. The first sentence has the idea of "until now" while the second sentence is talking only about that job in the past.

Ex. 15, p. 62: 1. have given 2. met, was, were 3. have seen 4. have dropped

Challenge, p. 63: Number 3 is incorrect. You cannot say, "I have written two letters last week" because you cannot use present perfect with "last week." Number 1 means that I have written two letters this week and the week is not over yet; I might write another letter. Number two means that I wrote two letters. The week may or may not be over. This sentence gives the idea or impression that I am not going to write any more letters this week. Number four is referring to a definite past time; the action is completely finished.

Ex. 16, p. 64: 1. past 2. present perfect 3. both 4. present perfect 5. past 6. both 7. present perfect 8. past 9. both 10. present perfect 11. both 12. both 13. past 14. past

Ex. 17, p. 64: 1. have gone 2. went 3. Have . . . eaten 4. did . . . eat 5. saw 6. have seen 7. have had 8. had 9. did. . . fly 10. have. . . flown

Ex. 18, p. 65: 1. called, were. . . —, was, have been 2. Have. . . worked, retired, did. . . work, worked, was 3. have. . . gone, have traveled, went, went, was, did. . . stay 4. have. . . been, were. . . —, was, had, did. . . work

Ex. 19, p. 66: 1. C 2. A 3. C 4. A 5. D 6. A 7. B 8. A

Ex. 20, p. 67: Part 1. 1. have. . . made 2. take, have decided, has. . . been, went, has traveled 3. is bleeding, was cutting, cut, Have . . . done (OR Did you ever do), has happened; Part 2. 1. wrong; change *met* to *known* 2. wrong; change *have gone* to *went* 3. correct 4. wrong; change *still* to *yet* 5. wrong; change *worked* to *has worked* 6. correct 7. wrong; change *has* to *has been* 8. correct

Quiz 1, p. 68: 1. was, been 2. made, made 3. forgot, forgotten 4. showed, shown 5. sat, sat 6. hit, hit 7. stole, stolen 8. took, taken 9. told, told 10. thought, thought 11. lost, lost 12. saw, seen 13. froze, frozen 14. sang, sung 15. slept, slept 16. left, left 17. swam, swum 18. taught, taught 19. broke, broken 20. ran, run

Quiz 2, p. 68: 1. said, said 2. wore, worn 3. wrote, written 4. began, begun 5. rode, ridden 6. spoke, spoken 7. bought, bought 8. caught, caught 9. drank, drunk 10. ate, eaten 11. chose, chosen 12. won, won 13. became, become 14. brought, brought 15. came, come 16. spent, spent 17. put, put 18. met, met 19. drove, driven 20. fell, fallen

Quiz 3, p. 69: 1. felt, felt 2. found, found 3. sold, sold 4. held, held 5. kept, kept 6. cost, cost 7. let, let 8. got, gotten 9. went, gone 10. built, built 11. did, done 12. lent, lent 13. sent, sent 14. read, read 15. knew, known 16. cut, cut 17. flew, flown 18. gave, given 19. had, had 20. understood, understood

Unit 5

Ex. 1, p. 73: 1. quickly 2. suddenly 3. sincerely 4. silently 5. happily 6. fast 7. punctually 8. well 9. enormously 10. wisely 11. hard 12. rapidly 13. poorly 14. furiously 15. sadly 16. promptly 17. carefully 18. badly 19. hugely 20. stupidly

Ex. 2, p. 73: 1. He works quietly. 2. She is a slow eater. 3. Mark swims very fast. 4. They sing well. 5. They are really careful workers. 6. Joy runs quickly 7. Tim is a fluent Thai speaker. 8. Keith isn't a good singer.

Ex. 3, p. 74: 1. good 2. rapid, nervous 3. dark, suddenly, hard 4. wise, poorly 5. nervously, correct 6. good, easy, beautifully 7. clear, high 8. rapidly, careful

Ex. 4, p. 74: 1. dangerously = dangerous 2. largely = large 3. specially = special 4. quiet = quietly 5. easy = easily 6. cleverly = clever

Ex. 5, p. 76: 1. by 2. with 3. with 4. by 5. with 6. by 7. with 8. with 9. by 10. with 11. by 12. by 13. with 14. by 15. by

Ex. 6, p. 76: 1. with, with 2. by, by, by 3. by, by 4. by, by 5. with, by

Ex. 7, p. 78: 1. saying 2. frying 3. counting 4. writing 5. stepping 6. taking 7. searching 8. working

Ex. 8, p. 78: Answers will vary.

Ex. 9, p. 78: 1. by practicing 2. to make 3. by not being 4. by repeating 5. by passing 6. to make 7. to find 8. to let

Ex. 10, p. 79: Answers will vary.

Ex. 11, p. 80: 1. D 2. C 3. A 4. B 5. D 6. D 7. C 8. B

Ex. 12, p. 81: Part 1. 1. By, by, by, with 2. by, by; Part 2. 1. quickly 2. well 3. hard 4. clear; Part 3. 1. correct 2. correct 3. correct 4. wrong; change *lately* to *late* 5. wrong; change *no* to *not* 6. wrong; change *fry* to *frying* 7. correct 8. correct

Unit 6

Ex. 1, p. 85: 1. with 2. of 3. for 4. to 5. on 6. about 7. to 8. to 9. to 10. at 11. to 12. of 13. to 14. for 15. of 16. for 17. on 18. about

Ex. 2, p. 85: 1. (look forward) to, (thank) for 2. (looking) for, (depends) on 3. (reminds) of, (agree) with, (think) of 4. (complain) about, (write) to, (listens) to, (wait) for

Ex. 3, p. 88: 1. good, E 2. scared, D 3. similar, F 4. happy, A 5. known, G 6. tired, C 7. tired, B 8. interested, H

Ex. 4, p. 88: 1. for 2. from 3. with 4. of 5. to 6. in 7. at 8. about

Ex. 5, p. 89: of: 1. afraid 2. ashamed 3. aware 4. composed 5. convinced 6. envious 7. full 8. guilty 9. innocent 10. jealous 11. made 12. proud 13. scared 14. sick 15. tired; *to:* 1. accustomed 2. harmful 3. married 4. opposed 5. polite 6. related 7. relevant 8. similar 9. used; *with:* 1. acquainted 2. bored 3. disappointed 4. done 5. familiar 6. finished 7. fed up 8. impressed 9. satisfied; *about:* 1. confused 2. crazy 3. curious 4. excited 5. happy 6. sorry 7. worried; *at:* 1. angry 2. bad 3. good 4. surprised; *for:* 1. famous 2. known 3. ready 4. responsible

Ex. 6, p. 90: 1. about 2. in (OR with) 3. at 4. of 5. of 6. of 7. of 8. to 9. of 10. for 11. with 12. to 13. in 14. of (OR from) 15. from 16. of 17. at 18. for 19. of 20. of 21. at 22. from 23. by (OR with) 24. to 25. to 26. with 27. for 28. with 29. with 30. about 31. of 32. about 33. for 34. to 35. of 36. in 37. to 38. about 39. about 40. with 41. of (OR from) 42. of 43. to 44. from 45. to 46. of 47. of 48. with 49. for 50. about 51. with 52. of 53. to 54. at

Ex. 7, p. 90: 1. used to 2. was used to 3. was used to 4. used to 5. used to 6. am used to 7. am not used to 8. used to

Challenge, p. 91: No, it's not correct. The correct sentence should be "When I was a kid, I used to have a dog . . ." This sentence is describing a past action that is no longer true because the dog has died, so we have to use *used to* + VERB.

Ex. 8, p. 91: Answers will vary.

Ex. 9, p. 92: Answers will vary.

Ex. 10, p. 93:

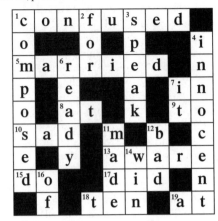

Ex. 11, p. 95: 1. A 2. D 3. B 4. A 5. D 6. C 7. B 8. B

Ex. 12, p. 96: Part 1. to, to, to, of, on, about; Part 2. 1. correct 2. correct 3. correct 4. wrong; change *with* to *on* 5. wrong; change *to* to *with* 6. wrong; change *buy* to *buying* 7. correct 8. wrong; wait for the bus

Unit 7

Ex. 1, p. 101: is done, is being done, was done, should be done, might be done, has to be done, is going to be done, was being done, has been done

Ex. 2, p. 102: 1. was invented 2. is written 3. will . . . find 4. has been sold 5. should be taken 6. are going to finish 7. finished 8. has been finished 9. were cooking 10. was built

Ex. 3, p. 102: 1. is mixed 2. took 3. is measured 4. be fried or baked, be served 5. take 6. was built 7. was fired, didn't attend 8. eat, is eaten 9. learned 10. is given

Ex. 4, p. 103: is looking, has taught, be interviewed, be sent, be called

Ex. 5, p. 103: 1. J 2. H 3. E 4. B 5. C 6. F 7. G 8. D 9. A 10. I

Ex. 6, p. 104: 1. correct 2. correct 3. wrong; is limited 4. wrong; died (omit *was*) 5. wrong; has been done 6. wrong; was discovered 7. correct 8. wrong; happened (omit *was*) 9. correct 10. wrong; marked (omit *was*) 11. wrong; omit the phrase "by builders" because it is not new information 12. correct

Challenge, p. 105: These verbs are intransitive verbs, and intransitive verbs only have one form. They do not have an active voice and a passive voice form. Intransitive verbs can never have *be* + PAST PARTICIPLE.

Ex. 7, p. 105: 1. are crowded 2. am interested 3. is . . . turned 4. are sealed 5. is done 6. am lost 7. am married 8. is frozen 9. was born 10. is stuck 11. is plugged 12. is located

Ex. 8, p. 107: 1. am opposed to 2. was excited about 3. is known for 4. am tired of 5. is not related to 6. be ashamed of 7. am scared of 8. Are . . . satisfied with 9. not be done with 10. is confused about 11. Are . . . acquainted with 12. are . . . worried about 13. is composed of 14. is tired from 15. was (OR am) exhausted from

Ex. 9, p. 108: Answers will vary.

Ex. 10, p. 110: 1. A. shocked B. shocking C. shocking 2. A. surprising B. surprised 3. A. perplexed B. perplexing C. perplexed 4. A. disgusted B. disgusting C. disgusted D. disgusting E. disgusting 5. A. confusing B. confusing C. confused D. confused, confusing

Ex. 11, p. 111: 1. confused 2. interested 3. interesting 4. terrified 5. fascinating 6. puzzled 7. tiring 8. depressed 9. embarrassed 10. amazing 11. interested 12. interesting 13. puzzled 14. fascinating 15. boring

Ex. 12, p. 113: 1. A 2. A 3. C 4. D 5. B 6. C 7. B 8. C

Ex. 13, p. 114: Part 1. Answers may vary. 1. are done (OR finished), has been purchased, have been made, are packed (OR have been packed) 2. is . . . done (OR finished), are finished (OR are done) 3. am worried, was . . . discovered, was . . . purchased, was chosen; Part 2. 1. wrong; omit the phrase "by me" because this information is not new 2. wrong; have been locked 3. wrong; were printed 4. wrong; happened 5. correct 6. correct 7. correct 8. wrong; should be returned 9. correct 10. correct

Unit 8

Ex. 1, p. 119: 1. that Joseph has 2. which we bought about seven years ago 3. who have children 4. that has always been very valuable 5. who live in Florida 6. that had raisins in them

Ex. 2, p. 119: 1. that/which 2. that/which, that/who 3. that/which, that/who, that/which 4. that/which, that/who 5. that/which, that/which

Ex. 3, p. 121:

1. Our history <u>teacher</u> usually <u>gives</u> tests
                   S1   V1
   (that <u>have</u> multiple choice questions).
     S2 V2

2. <u>Tests</u> (that <u>have</u> multiple choice questions)
   S1   S2 V2
   <u>are</u> not so difficult.
   V1

3. <u>Drinking</u> milk (<u>which</u> <u>doesn't have</u> any fat in
   S1   S2   V2
   it) <u>is</u> healthier than drinking regular milk.
     V1

4. <u>I</u> just <u>can't stand</u> the taste of milk (<u>which</u>
   S1   V1   S2
   <u>doesn't have</u> any fat in it).
     V1

5. The <u>man</u> (<u>who</u> <u>won</u> the marathon) <u>is</u> from Kenya.
      S1   S2 V2   V1

6. <u>Everyone</u> <u>took</u> photos of the man (<u>who</u> <u>won</u> the
   S1   V1   S2 V2
   marathon).

Ex. 4, p. 121: 1. who wrote a popular novel (OR that) 2. that is in a blue box (OR which) 3. that is on Van Avenue (OR which) 4. who became president in 1993 (OR that) 5. who teaches chemistry at 9 o'clock (OR that) 6. who failed the test (OR that)

Ex. 5, p. 123: 1. that I took is expensive (OR which, ∅) 2. that Samantha recommended (OR which, ∅) 3. that Ben bought (OR which, ∅) 4. that Channel 7 gave was wrong (OR which, ∅) 5. that Lynn made (OR which, ∅) 6. that we bought was wet (OR which, ∅)

Ex. 6, p. 123: 1. The young woman wrote a popular novel that (which) deals with crime in a rural town. 2. The young woman wrote a popular novel that (which, ∅) all my friends have read. 3. This is the letter that (which) was in a green envelope. 4. This is the letter that (which, ∅) my cousin wrote. 5. Did you buy the TV that (which) was on sale? 6. Did you buy the TV that (which, ∅) you wanted? 7. Do you understand the question that (which) is at the top of the page? 8. Do you understand the question that (which, ∅) you missed?

Challenge, p. 124: Have you seen the movie that is about a president who was kidnapped by terrorists?

Ex. 7, p. 124: 1. The student (<u>that</u>) <u>the teacher called on</u> is from Venezuela. 2. The student <u>that arrived late</u> is from Venezuela. 3. Do you ever watch the program <u>that is on channel 8 at 3 P.M.</u>? 4. What is the name of the cologne (<u>that</u>) <u>you like so much</u>? 5. I don't like the color of the dress (<u>that</u>) <u>she bought</u>. 6. The people <u>who arrived even a little late</u> couldn't get good seats. 7. I hate to eat fish <u>that has a lot of bones</u>. 8. The politician (<u>whom</u>) <u>most people admire now in our state</u> is a woman. 9. My friend said, "The woman <u>who is speaking now</u> is the CEO at a huge corporation in Miami." 10. My friend said, "The woman (<u>who</u>) <u>she is speaking to</u> is the CEO at a huge corporation in Miami." 11. I was reading a book (<u>that</u>) <u>Becky gave me</u> when I fell asleep. 12. Hank thinks that we should not buy products <u>which contain leather</u>.

Ex. 8, p. 125: 1. the weather report I saw an hour ago said rain 2. the cookies Publix makes are not too sweet OR Publix makes cookies that are not too sweet 3. How was the test you had yesterday?

4. Did you like the rice dish Lee cooked? What do you call those vegetables that were in it? 5. Did you speak to the doctor Mary spoke to? The doctor I spoke to had red hair.

Challenge, p. 126: It probably occurred in something written because of the word *whom*. Remember that in informal conversation, most speakers will use *who* instead of *whom*.

Ex. 9, p. 127: 1. I talked to the man whose son is in my art class. 2. The students whose last name begins with A are listed on the first page. 3. The boy whose drawing won first prize in the contest was so happy. 4. We might play tennis with the woman whose father we know. 5. We might play tennis with the woman whose father won the club tournament. 6. Pilots whose contracts begin in January will make less money.

Ex. 10, p. 128: 1. I talked to the man (who was) standing in front of the supermarket. 2. I asked the boys (that were) playing tennis what the time was. 3. Have you seen the movie that tells the story of the *Titanic*'s maiden journey? 4. The Chinese restaurant (that is) near my house has great egg drop soup. 5. We chose three of the sandwiches (which were) on the table. 6. He was talking on the phone when someone knocked on the door. 7. I always mix up words (that are) spelled "ei" with words (that are) spelled "ie." 8. Plants that can stand hot, dry summers grow well in this area of the country. 9. Only two of the boys who wanted to work overtime were able to do it. 10. The child (who is) playing with the cat is my little sister.

Ex. 11, p. 128: Answers will vary.

Ex. 12, p. 129: Answers will vary.

Ex. 13, p. 130: Answers will vary.

Ex. 14, p. 131: 1. A 2. B 3. C 4. B 5. D 6. A 7. C 8. D

Ex. 15, p. 132: Part 1. One of the most interesting countries <u>(that) you can visit</u> is Venezuela. Venezuela is in the northern part of South America. The countries <u>which border on Venezuela</u> are Brazil, Colombia, and Guyana. Venezuela has four distinct geographical regions. The first region is the Guiana Highlands. This area is an extensive area of high plains and plateaus <u>that extends from the Orinoco River to the Brazilian border</u>. Next, the area <u>that lies between the Orinoco River and the Andes Mountains</u> is called the llanos. The llanos is a section of flat plains. The third area of this country is the hot and humid coastal plain. This is the area <u>which contains oil</u>. It includes Lake Maracaibo and the Orinoco River delta. Finally, the region <u>which is located in the southwestern corner</u> <u>of the country</u> includes the high peaks of the Andes Mountains. Although all the people in Venezuela speak Spanish, the people <u>who live in these four areas</u> speak slightly differently from the people in the other areas. For example, the people <u>who live in the Andes region of the country</u> speak very differently from other Venezuelans. Part 2. that/which, who/that, that/which/Ø/, that/which, that/which/Ø/, that/which, that/which/Ø/, that/who/whom/Ø/; Part 3. 1. wrong; owners who (OR that) want 2. correct 3. correct 4. correct 5. wrong; that I wrote (omit *it*) 6. wrong; woman whose son 7. correct

Unit 9

Ex. 1, p. 137: 1. to do 2. doing 3. doing 4. to do 5. to do 6. to do 7. to do 8. to do 9. doing 10. to do 11. doing 12. doing 13. doing 14. doing 15. to do 16. to do 17. to do 18. doing 19. doing 20. to do 21. to do

Ex. 2, p. 138: 1. doing 2. to do 3. doing 4. doing 5. doing 6. doing 7. to do 8. to do 9. doing 10. to do

Ex. 3, p. 138: 1. to go, going, to leave, to leave, to leave, going, to avoid, driving, to go, doing 2. eating, to cook, to eat, to serve, to have, to keep on, eating 3. taking, to go, to go, to go, going, to go, to go, to let, to go, sightseeing

Ex. 4, p. 140: Answers will vary.

Ex. 5, p. 141: Answers will vary.

Ex. 6, p. 142: 1. to change 2. counting 3. to get 4. smoking 5. taking 6. giving 7. dancing 8. buying

Ex. 7, p. 146: 1. C 2. made them do 3. ask him to call 4. C 5. C 6. got everyone to agree 7. would like their kids to eat 8. allow me to change 9. C 10. persuade him to go 11. told you to do 12. C

Ex. 8, p. 147: Answers will vary.

Ex. 9, p. 147: 1. B 2. B 3. C 4. D 5. B 6. D 7. B 8. C

Ex. 10, p. 149: Part 1. going, going, to see, to go, going, writing, going, writing, to use, to accept, do, to write, to stop, writing, doing; Part 2. 1. correct 2. wrong; Driving there takes ("To drive" is possible but rare.) 3. correct 4. correct 5. correct; wrong; know how to swim

Unit 10

Ex. 1, p. 152: 1. Why did she drive to the mall? To pick up her children's photos. In order to pick up her children's photos. For her children's photos. 2. Why are some kids collecting money? To help the storm victims. In order to help the storm victims. For the storm victims. 3. Why does Mr. McDowell usually go to that deli? To get fresh bread. In order to get fresh bread. For fresh bread.

Ex. 2, p. 153: 1. for, to 2. for, to 3. to, to 4. to, for 5. for, to

Ex. 3, p. 156: 1. and Ken did too, and so did Ken 2. and his cousin is too, and so is his cousin 3. and Chile does too, and so does Chile 4. and that plane can too, and so can that plane 5. and Wanda does too, and so does Wanda 6. and Bo does too, and so does Bo

Challenge, p. 156: The second student is correct. You cannot use *have* or *has* here because *have* is the main verb in this sentence. When *have* is an auxiliary verb, then you can repeat *have*.

Ex. 4, p. 157: 1. and Ted doesn't either, and neither does Ted 2. and you shouldn't either, and neither should you 3. and the Sawyers didn't either, and neither did the Sawyers 4. and science class isn't either, and neither is science class 5. and I didn't either, and neither did I 6. and I don't either, and neither do I

Ex. 5, p. 157: 1. but 2. but 3. and 4. but 5. and 6. and 7. but 8. and 9. and 10. and

Ex. 6, p. 158: 1. do too 2. neither did 3. is too 4. so is 5. isn't 6. couldn't either 7. does too 8. neither does 9. does 10. doesn't either 11. so does 12. has too 13. so do 14. is too 15. isn't

Ex. 7, p. 159: Answers will vary.

Ex. 8, p. 160: Answers will vary.

Ex. 9, p. 161: 1. so, However, so 2. so 3. so, However, Therefore 4. so, however

Ex. 10, p. 162:

1. The little boy wanted to buy a gift for his mother; however, he didn't have enough money. (OR mother. However,)

2. Health care in the U.S. is very expensive, so many people don't have any health insurance.

3. Health care in the U.S. is not free; however, in Canada the situation is very different. (OR free. However,)

4. Vietnam was a French colony for many years; therefore, French is spoken in some parts. (OR years. Therefore,)

5. The price of tickets for the concert is $50; however, the tickets are selling very quickly. (OR $50. However,)

6. The flight was overbooked; therefore, some passengers were denied boarding. (OR overbooked. Therefore,)

7. Yvonne cooked a huge pot of stew so everyone would be able to eat some at the party.

8. Yvonne cooked a huge pot of stew, so everyone was able to eat some at the party.

Ex. 11, p. 163:

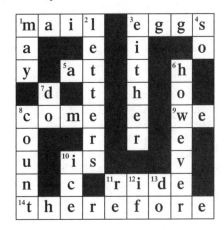

Ex. 12, p. 165: 1. D 2. C 3. A 4. D 5. D 6. A 7. B 8. B

Ex. 13, p. 166: Part 1. 1. to, so did 2. Therefore, However, so 3. however, However, in order to; Part 2. 1. correct 2. wrong; but 3. correct 4. wrong; does too 5. wrong; doesn't 6. wrong; to 7. correct 8. correct

Unit 11

Ex. 1, p. 170: 1. B 2. A 3. A 4. B 5. B 6. A 7. B 8. A 9. A 10. A 11. B 12. B

Ex. 2, p. 171: 1. to 2. for 3. to 4. for 5. to 6. for 7. to 8. for 9. for 10. for

Ex. 3, p. 171: 1. for me 2. to me 3. for me 4. for me 5. to me 6. for me 7. to me 8. to me 9. for me 10. for me

Ex. 4, p. 171: 1. for 2. to 3. for 4. to 5. to 6. for 7. for 8. to 9. for 10. to 11. for 12. to 13. to 14. for 15. to 16. to 17. for 18. for 19. for 20. to

Ex. 5, p. 172: 1. to 2. to 3. to 4. for 5. for 6. for

Ex. 6, p. 173: 1. 2 2. 1 3. 2 4. 1 5. 2

Ex. 7, p. 174: 1. He's going to ask the teacher a question. 2. They charged Mr. Hernandez twenty dollars for a new shirt. 3. She saved Joe ten dollars by telling him about the sale at the store. 4. We asked the man the time of day. 5. The old man wished us a happy holiday. 6. The new red bicycle cost me over one hundred dollars. 7. That store charged her fifteen dollars for some cotton socks. 8. All of us wished Zoe a safe journey.

Ex. 8, p. 175: 1. That new dress cost Maria seventy dollars. 2. Can you ask the pilot a question? 3. How much did Sears charge you? 4. I save myself a lot of money by not smoking. 5. My uncle wished me good luck on the test tomorrow. 6. One student asked the teacher three difficult questions yesterday.

Ex. 9, p. 176: 1. AB 2. AB 3. AB 4. AB 5. AB 6. AB 7. AB 8. AB 9. AB 10. AB

Ex. 10, p. 177: 1. Warren wrote a letter to Molly. 2. I always read the newspaper to my brother. 3. We show our artwork to the class. 4. She teaches new words to the students. 5. Please tell the good news to Rose. 6. I'm going to sell my bike to Daria. 7. I usually lend my car to Paul. 8. Did she bring another apple to the teacher? 9. Would you please take the food to your father? 10. He passed the pepper to me.

Ex. 11, p. 177: 1. I didn't teach Kim golf. 2. He showed Diane the map. 3. He brought me some flowers. 4. Please lend Carl the money. 5. Did you write your sister a thank-you note? 6. I sold Lisa my old stove. 7. Pass Alan the test. 8. She is going to read me the poem. 9. Take Ms. Brady the money. 10. I never tell my parents lies.

Ex. 12, p. 178: 1. I'm going to get some tea for Joanne. 2. She found a job for Andy. 3. He made a sandwich for the girl. 4. The teacher got a pencil for the student. 5. My brother did a favor for me.

Ex. 13, p. 178: 1. I made the students some coffee. 2. Mr. Erwin got his wife some nice flowers. 3. He found me a key. 4. They did me a big favor. 5. They didn't buy me a ticket.

Ex. 14, p. 179: 1. AB 2. B 3. A 4. AB 5. AB 6. B 7. AB 8. A 9. A 10. A 11. AB 12. AB 13. A 14. A 15. AB 16. B 17. AB 18. A 19. AB 20. A

Ex. 15, p. 180: 1. A 2. A 3. AB 4. A 5. AB 6. AB 7. A 8. AB 9. AB 10. A 11. AB 12. A

Ex. 16, p. 180: 1. for me 2. me 3. for me 4. for me 5. to me 6. me 7. to me 8. to me 9. for me 10. to me 11. me 12. to me 13. me 14. for me 15. to me 16. me 17. me 18. me 19. for me 20. for me 21. me 22. for me 23. me 24. me

Challenge, p. 181: The two sentences are wrong because both objects are pronouns. In English, you cannot put two pronoun objects next to each other. You can say, "I gave it to him," but you cannot say, "I gave him it."

Ex. 17, p. 181: 1. explained 2. made 3. show 4. sends 5. pass 6. pronounced 7. take 8. sent 9. bring 10. get 11. lend 12. found 13. tells 14. wished 15. mentioned 16. give

Ex. 18, p. 182: A. buy Sammy a gift, buy a gift for Sammy; explain the new word to me; introduce her to me; wish Sandy happy birthday; say hello to me; give the cards to me, give me the cards; show my new computer to them, show them my new computer; close the door for me; B. do the work for us; make a cake for me, make me a cake; wish us good luck; describe your new house to me; explain the directions to us; open the door for me; take these books to Mr. Lee, take Mr. Lee these books; find the girl a chair, find a chair for the girl

Ex. 19, p. 184: 1. C 2. C 3. B 4. D 5. B 6. B 7. A 8. C

Ex. 20, p. 185: Part 1. 1. —, to 2. —, — 3. to, for, for, —, for 4. for; Part 2. 1. lend 2. mentioned 3. pass 4. tells; Part 3. 1. wrong; the police officer the location 2. correct 3. correct 4. wrong; for me 5. wrong; told you the news about Laura

Unit 12

Ex. 1, p. 188: 1. picked her up 2. gave it away 3. went over it 4. handed it in 5. ran into them (at the mall) 6. ran out of it 7. came across it 8. am looking after him 9. are counting on them 10. has filled it out 11. turn them on 12. calls on me

Ex. 2, p. 188: 1. was waiting 2. ate, wrote 3. woke, were barking 4. did . . . arrive 5. was sleeping, hit, did . . . do, jumped, put 6. was raining, had 7. got, was playing, was watching, got, weren't doing 8. saw, was riding, saw, was doing

Ex. 3, p. 189: 1. did you work, was 2. Have you ever gone (OR Did you ever go), went, was, went, was it, had 3. have already seen (OR already saw), did you like, was it, thought, was 4. have known, did you meet

Ex. 4, p. 190: 1. beautiful, by picking 2. smart, well 3. with 4. opening, slowly 5. to make 6. by, by

Ex. 5, p. 191: 1. to, from 2. to, for, from 3. of, about, of, to 4. about, for, in, to 5. for, of

Ex. 6, p. 192: 1. want, do, be completed, be included, fill, help, be filled, is preferred, use 2. is considered, don't like 3. are spoken, is spoken, speak, is spoken 4. is taken, has been calculated, have done

Ex. 7, p. 193: 1. that, which 2. that, which, — 3. who, that 4. that, which 5. that, which, — 6. that, which, — 7. that, who (conversation), whom (formal), — 8. that, which, — 9. that, which, — 10. that, which 11. that, which, — 12. that, which

Ex. 8, p. 194: 1. to take 2. to eat 3. taking 4. eating 5. to go 6. to eat 7. going 8. taking 9. to get 10. to order 11. to believe 12. to eat 13. to change 14. to order 15. listening

Ex. 9, p. 195: 1. so, does "bread" 2. to 3. Therefore 4. either 5. got 6. Therefore 7. either 8. to 9. didn't want 10. did 11. so 12. so is 13. isn't 14. can speak 15. but I haven't

Ex. 10, p. 196: 1. to 2. for 3. for 4. to, to 5. to 6. to 7. — 8. to 9. to 10. — 11. for 12. to

Ex. 11, p. 196: Errors: 2. Could you please pass the salt to me? (OR Could you please pass me the salt?) 6. I didn't have my watch, so I asked Nick the time. 8. All of us sang "Happy Birthday" to wish Sarah good luck on her new year. 10. I'm going to get some tea for us now. (OR I'm going to get us some tea.) I'll be right back.

Final Test

Name________________________________ Date ______________

This test has 22 questions. You will receive 1 point for circling the error and 1 point for correcting the error. Perfect score = 44.
Your score: ____/44 = ____%
(70% minimum recommended for passing)

Each sentence contains one error. Circle the error and write a correction on the line. If your answer is long, you may write it above the sentence.

example: ____have____ I (has) a book.

Part 1

1. ____________________ Secretary in my office just had a baby boy.
2. ____________________ A long time ago, doctors called patients on at home.
3. ____________________ An old woman knocked on my door when I took a bath.
4. ____________________ Have you ever flew on a flight across the Pacific Ocean?
5. ____________________ She found out the price of the hotel room by call up a travel agent.
6. ____________________ When I was a little kid, I was used to hate onions, but now I love them.
7. ____________________ The most confused problem that we face today is how to deal with young people who commit really serious crimes.
8. ____________________ Can someone tell me the name of the leader which led Britain during World War I?
9. ____________________ My aunt's food was bad, but I pretended enjoy eating it.
10. ____________________ This dictionary doesn't have example sentences which are written in simple English. However, we decided not to buy it.
11. ____________________ May I ask a question about this schedule to you?

Part 2

1. _____ All new employees at this company has to have a driver's
license.

2. _____ Ellen tore up the letter and then threw away it.

3. _____ When Jill called me, I ate dinner.

4. _____ I have met Roger at a meeting in Ohio about six or
seven years ago.

5. _____ When the dog appeared, the cat ran away very quick.

6. _____ All of the passengers were worried for the strange noise
of the jet engine.

7. _____ Unfortunately, the number of smokers in this country is
grown.

8. _____ The little boy who wearing a dark blue coat is my
nephew.

9. _____ For some reason, Kevin refused to consider to postpone
his trip.

10. _____ The best time for see the animals here is very early in the
morning.

11. _____ My daughter was so proud when she showed her art me.

Diagnostic Test

Name_____ Date_____

Directions: Mark an X on the letter of the correct answer. Mark all answers on this sheet.

					TEACHER ONLY Number wrong (0, 1, 2)

1a.   (A) (B) (C) (D)   1b.   (A) (B) (C) (D)   _____

2a.   (A) (B) (C) (D)   2b.   (A) (B) (C) (D)   _____

3a.   (A) (B) (C) (D)   3b.   (A) (B) (C) (D)   _____

4a.   (A) (B) (C) (D)   4b.   (A) (B) (C) (D)   _____

5a.   (A) (B) (C) (D)   5b.   (A) (B) (C) (D)   _____

6a.   (A) (B) (C) (D)   6b.   (A) (B) (C) (D)   _____

7a.   (A) (B) (C) (D)   7b.   (A) (B) (C) (D)   _____

8a.   (A) (B) (C) (D)   8b.   (A) (B) (C) (D)   _____

9a.   (A) (B) (C) (D)   9b.   (A) (B) (C) (D)   _____

10a. (A) (B) (C) (D)   10b. (A) (B) (C) (D)   _____

11a. (A) (B) (C) (D)   11b. (A) (B) (C) (D)   _____

Diagnostic Test Questions

1a. "How did you like the sandwich? I've made a lot, so do you want _____ one?"

"Yes, please."

(A) other

(C) others

(B) another

(D) the other

2a. "Where did you get that dictionary?"

"I came _____ at Wilson's Bookstore on Fletcher Avenue."

(A) up it

(C) across it

(B) it up

(D) it across

3a. "Did you hear the crash yesterday?"

"Are you kidding? Of course I did. When the police car _____ into the bank, I was actually working inside."

(A) crashed

(C) crashing

(B) was crashing

(D) going to crash

4a. "Do you like living in this town?"

"Well, I _____ here for over twenty years, so it's my home really."

(A) am living

(C) was living

(B) live

(D) have lived

5a. "How did you get the bathroom floor so white?"

"I washed the floor a couple of times _____ an extra strong cleaner."

(A) by

(C) with

(B) by using

(D) with using

6a. "So how was your score on the college entrance exam?"

"It wasn't so bad, but I _____ the results because I was expecting a higher score."

(A) was disappointed with   (C) disappointed with

(B) was disappointed for   (D) disappointed for

7a. "Hey, I just heard that Randy lost his job at the computer store."

"Yes, that's right. He _____ training sessions."

(A) fired because he didn't attend   (C) was fired because he didn't attend

(B) fired because he wasn't attended   (D) was fired because he wasn't attended

8a. This is the photo _____ on the day that President Kennedy was killed.

(A) that took it the young man   (C) that took the young man

(B) that the young man took it   (D) that the young man took

9a. "I've been late to work every day this week. The traffic on Bern Street is terrible."

"If you'd like _____ late, then why don't you use Young Avenue instead?"

(A) avoiding being   (C) avoiding to be

(B) to avoid being   (D) to avoid to be

10a. "I need to get a job really soon. What do you think I should do?"

"_____ a really good job, you need to put together a good resume."

(A) For getting   (C) To get

(B) By getting   (D) For get

11a. "Could you please _____ me the menu?"

"Certainly."

(A) suggest   (C) say

(B) open   (D) pass

1b. "My tooth hurts. I don't know how much longer I can stand this."

"Then you have no choice. You _____ to see the dentist right away."

(A) should   (C) must

(B) could   (D) have

2b. I tried to figure _____ the answers to this puzzle, but I couldn't do it.

(A) out   (C) away

(B) on   (D) up

3b. "_____ the baseball game on TV when the lights went out last night?"

"Yes! What a bad time for the lights to go out!"

(A) Did you watch   (C) Did you were watching

(B) Were you watching   (D) Were you watched

4b. "I am going to attend a meeting in Mexico City next month."

"I'm sure you'll have a good time. I've been there several times. In fact, I

_____ to Mexico City on business just last month."

(A) went   (C) have gone

(B) was   (D) have been

5b. If you want to learn to paint _____, you have to practice a lot.

(A) beautiful pictures accurate   (C) beautifully pictures accurately

(B) beautiful pictures accurately   (D) beautifully pictures accurate

6b. "You start your new job tomorrow, right?"

"Yes, and I'm so excited _____ with everyone there."

(A) about work   (C) about working

(B) for work   (D) for working

7b. "Smoking causes more preventable deaths here than anything else."

"I know. The sale of cigarettes should _____ immediately."

(A) prohibit

(C) be prohibited

(B) prohibited

(D) be prohibiting

8b. "Do you know the name of the woman _____ car caught fire in the parking lot?"

"No, I don't. Wow, that was certainly a terrible thing for her. She was lucky to survive."

(A) whose

(C) whom

(B) which

(D) who

9b. "Why did the police shoot the bank robber?"

"The bank robber was shooting at the police. The captain ordered _____ him if he kept on shooting at them."

(A) that they shoot

(C) them shoot

(B) them to shoot

(D) to them to shoot

10b. The first store we went to didn't have any good furniture for sale, and _____.

(A) so does this store

(C) this store does too

(B) neither does this store

(D) this store doesn't neither

11b. "Is that a new tie?"

"Yes, my daughter gave _____ yesterday."

(A) this tie for me

(C) this tie me

(B) to me this tie

(D) me this tie